UNIT A

Systems in Living Things

Theme: Systems

THINK LIKE A SCIENTIST

THINK LIKE A SCIENTIST

BREATHING SPACE

You are looking inside the gas-exchange organ of the human body—the lung. In this magnified image, you can see some of the many tiny sacs (the dark spaces) that fill with air each time you breathe. The orange-colored spheres are red blood cells, which pick up oxygen from the lungs. The lungs are just one of the many kinds of organs that work together in the body to keep you alive and healthy.

Do a Test • Record and Analyze • Draw Conclusions • Make Observations • Ask a Question • Make a Hypothesis • Plan and Do a Test

Ask a Question • Make a Hypothesis • Plan and Do a Test • Record and Analyze • Draw Conclusio

THINK LIKE A SCIENTIST

Questioning In this unit you'll study the life processes and systems of plants and animals. You'll investigate questions such as these.

- What Is a Living Thing?
- How Does the Respiratory System Work?

Observing, Testing, Hypothesizing In the Activity "Lung Power," you'll observe a working model of a lung. You'll also hypothesize what happens in your body when you breathe.

Researching In the Resource "Breathing Basics," you'll gather more information about the parts of the respiratory system and how the parts work together.

Drawing Conclusions After you've completed your investigations, you'll draw conclusions about what you've learned— and get new ideas.

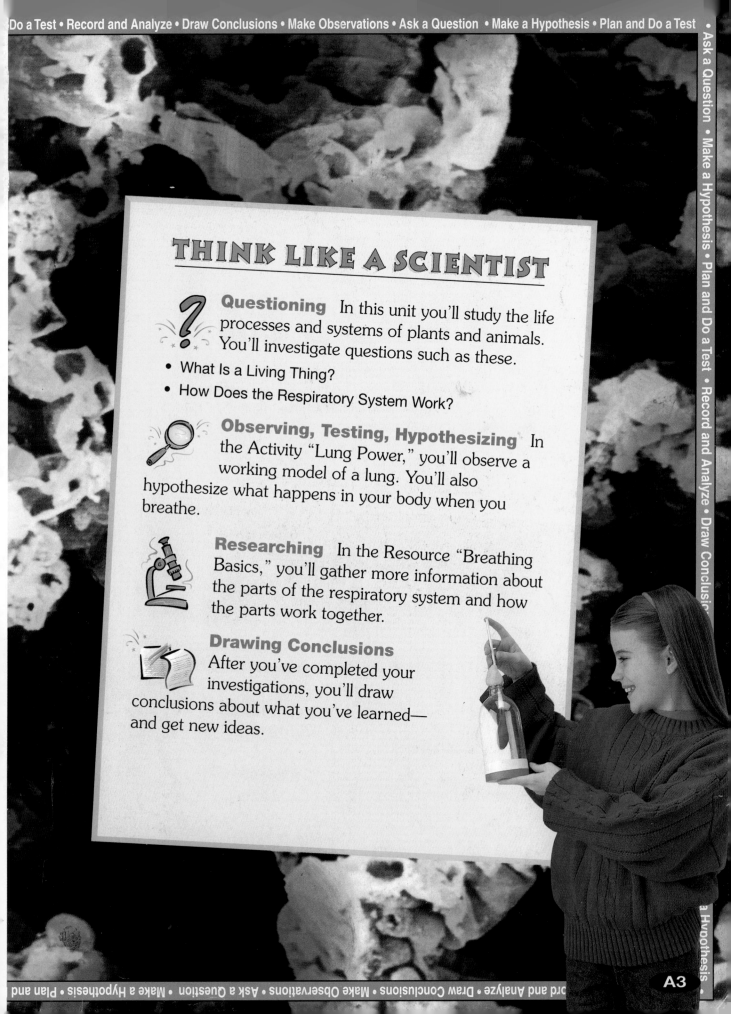

LIFE PROCESSES

How can you tell the difference between a living thing and a nonliving thing? What are the parts of a plant? of an animal? Which systems of living things allow them to eat, grow, and repair injured parts? In this chapter you'll explore the answers to these questions.

Connecting to Science
ARTS

Topiary Artist Linda Rodriguez has an unusual job. She creates animals from plants! The animals that Linda Rodriguez creates are sculptures called topiaries (tō′pē er ēz). She is a topiary artist for the San Diego Zoo. Her job is to make sculptures of lions, tigers, bears, and other zoo animals. She makes her sculptures in two different ways. Sometimes she allows bushes to grow. Then she snips the bushes into different animal shapes. Other times she begins with a hollow mesh frame. She packs the frame tightly with moss and then roots ivy in the moss. As the ivy grows, Linda Rodriguez cuts and trains the growing plants to the shape of the frame. Her knowledge of living things—both plants and animals—helps make her creations realistic as well as fun!

Coming Up

◀ Linda Rodriguez sculpts an ivy-covered animal.

WHAT IS A LIVING THING?

Can you tell whether something is alive just by looking at it? Seeds appear lifeless, but they can grow into giant trees. Some silk flowers look very much alive. Yet, when you touch them, you know they are fakes. In this investigation you'll explore the main features that make living things different from nonliving things.

Activity

Alive or Not?

What information do you need to determine if something is alive or not? In this activity you'll become a detective. Your job will be to ask the right questions to learn if something is a genuine living thing or if it is a clever fake.

Procedure

1. Look at the pairs of photos on this page and on A7. You'll need to decide which photo in each pair shows something that is alive.

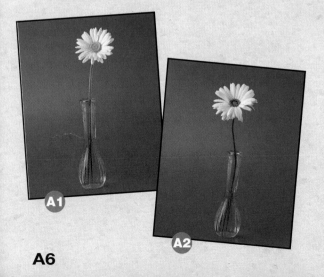

2. **Observe** each pair of photos carefully. In your *Science Notebook,* **record** a general description of the objects in each pair. Be sure to identify both the letter and number of the object you are describing.

3. For each pair of objects, look for clues that suggest which of the pair is alive. **Talk with your group** and together **brainstorm** a list of questions about each pair of objects. The questions should help you decide whether each object is alive or not.

4. Make a list of tests you could carry out to find out whether the objects are alive or not. **Describe** the tests you would carry out for each pair of objects.

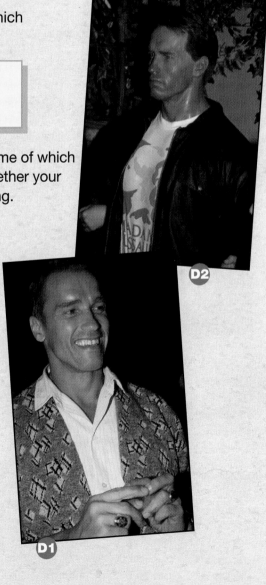

Analyze and Conclude

1. In your *Science Notebook,* make a chart that lists the tests your group came up with for step 4. In the chart, explain how each test would help you know which object in each pair was alive and which was not.

See **SCIENCE** and **MATH TOOLBOX** page H11 if you need to review *Making a Chart to Organize Data.*

2. Have one member of your group list six things, some of which are living and some of which are nonliving. Decide whether your tests could help identify each thing as living or nonliving.

3. Based on the results of this activity, **make a generalization** about what characteristics, or traits, distinguish living things from nonliving things.

A7

Activity

Observing Plant Cells

The part of the onion you eat is actually a ball of leaves called a bulb. Onions, like all plants, are made up of basic units called cells. Look at an onion through a microscope to see what plant cells look like.

MATERIALS

- goggles
- onion
- tweezers
- microscope slide
- iodine solution
- toothpick
- cover slip
- microscope
- *Science Notebook*

SafETY /////

Wear goggles during this activity. Be careful when handling glass slides. Iodine will stain clothing and is poisonous if swallowed.

Procedure

1. Take a section of an onion and snap it in half. A thin piece of skin should separate from the section. Peel this piece off with tweezers, as shown below.

2. Place the onion skin on a microscope slide. Add one drop of iodine solution. Use a toothpick to smooth out the wrinkles. Cover the onion skin with a cover slip.

 See **SCIENCE** *and* **MATH TOOLBOX** *page H2 if you need to review* **Using a Microscope.**

Step 1

Step 2

3. Observe the onion skin under a microscope at low power and draw what you see in your *Science Notebook*. Then observe the skin under high power and draw what you see.

Step 3

4. The small circular structure that turned deep red inside the onion cell is called a nucleus (no͞o′klē əs). Label the nucleus in your drawings.

5. The boundary of the cell is called the cell wall. Label the cell wall in your drawing.

Analyze and Conclude

1. Like all living things, plants are made of cells. Describe the appearance of the cells that you observed.

2. A cell wall is found only in plant cells, not in animal cells. Hypothesize what job the cell wall has.

3. Suppose you looked through a microscope at cells from an unknown living thing. How could you tell whether you were looking at plant cells or animal cells?

INVESTIGATE FURTHER!

EXPERIMENT

Use a dropper to add two drops of water to a microscope slide. Place a single *Elodea* leaf in the water and cover it with a cover slip. Observe the leaf under a microscope's low power. Then study the leaf under high power and make a sketch of what you see. Describe any structures that you see in the leaf cell that you did not see in the onion cell in the activity. Infer what the functions of such structures are, based on the leaf's role in a plant.

It's Alive!

Reading Focus How do plants and animals differ in the way they carry out their life processes?

Living things are all around you. Every tree, every blade of grass, and every insect is alive. Scientists have found life on the highest mountains and in the deepest oceans. They have discovered life on bare rocks and in snowbanks.

Alive—Or Not?

As the activity on pages A6 and A7 shows, it can be difficult to tell whether an object is living or nonliving. Montana moss agate (ag'it), for example, has fooled many people. This rock contains green streaks that "grow" and are often mistaken for moss or roots. The streaks are actually mineral crystals. The crystals grow, but not the way that living things grow.

▲ **Moss agate, a kind of rock. Moss agate as seen through a microscope (*inset*) .**

Look closely at the objects in the ocean beach scene below. Which ones do you think are alive?

Many of the seemingly lifeless objects in this scene are really alive. ▼

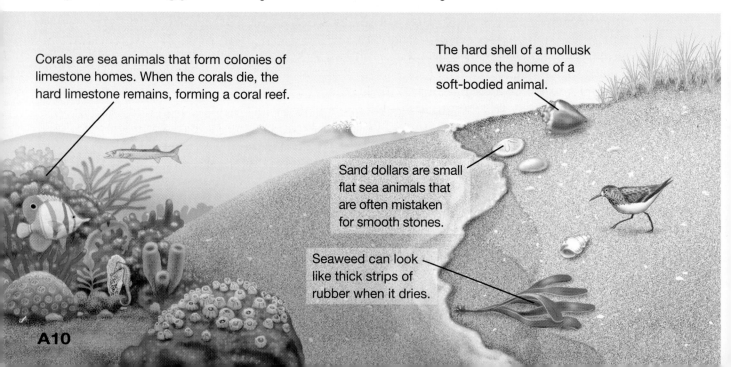

Corals are sea animals that form colonies of limestone homes. When the corals die, the hard limestone remains, forming a coral reef.

The hard shell of a mollusk was once the home of a soft-bodied animal.

Sand dollars are small flat sea animals that are often mistaken for smooth stones.

Seaweed can look like thick strips of rubber when it dries.

Life Processes

A **cell** is the basic unit of living things. Some simple organisms consist of only one cell. Most living things are composed of many cells. These cells work together to carry out the life processes of that organism. **Life processes** are the functions that a living thing must carry out in order to stay alive and produce more of its own kind.

Living things, as you have seen, can sometimes look like they are nonliving. What trait separates living from non-living things? A living thing carries out basic life processes. For example, all living things must take in **nutrients** (nōō′trē ənts), which are substances that are needed for an organism to live and grow. Living things also increase in size and change in other ways during their life cycle.

The basic life processes are listed in the table that follows. Examples are given of how plants and animals carry out these processes. Look for ways that the life processes are alike and different in plants and animals.

Comparing Life Processes

Life Process	Plants	Animals
Taking in materials, such as nutrients and gases	Take in carbon dioxide from air and take in water and minerals from soil	Take in oxygen from the air and nutrients from the food they eat
Releasing energy in food to carry out life processes	Release energy from the food they make	Release energy from the food they eat
Giving off wastes	Give off oxygen as a waste product of food making; also give off carbon dioxide and water as waste products	Give off carbon dioxide and other waste products
Reacting to surroundings	Stems grow toward a source of light; roots grow toward a source of water.	Move to find food, water, and suitable temperatures
Growing and developing	Increase in size and undergo change during their life cycle	Increase in size and undergo change during their life cycle
Reproducing	Most form seeds that result from the union of male and female reproductive cells	Produce offspring that result from the union of male and female reproductive cells

Cells—The Building Blocks of Life

Reading Focus How do plant and animal cells differ from each other?

Recall that the cell is the basic unit that makes up living things. It is the building block of both plants and animals. Each cell contains various parts, each with its own unique role in keeping the cell alive.

Comparing Plant and Animal Cells

The activity on pages A8 and A9 shows plant cells. Plant and animal cells have certain parts in common. There are also some cell parts that are unique to, or occur only in, plant cells. Other cell parts are unique to animal cells.

The drawings on page A13 show a typical plant cell and a typical animal cell. Notice the colored numbers pointing to the cell parts. You'll see that some parts are found in both kinds of cells. Some parts are found only in plant cells; others are found only in animal cells.

Cells Work Together

How do cells work together to form a living thing? Similar cells working together form a **tissue** (tish'$\overline{oo}$). Muscle cells, for example, work with many other muscle cells to form muscle tissue. Different types of tissues work together to form an **organ**, such as the liver, heart, stomach, and small intestine.

In plants, as in animals, there are tissues and organs. For example, cells containing green pigment work together to form leaf tissue. Groups of tissues together form plant organs, such as the leaf, stem, and root. Each organ performs a certain function that helps the plant, or animal, maintain life.

Groups of organs work together to form an **organ system**, such as the circulatory system. The circulatory system brings oxygen to each cell of the body and removes waste products in animals. Together, groups of organ systems form a living thing, such as a pine tree, a cat, or a person.

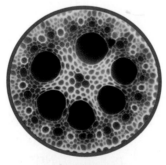

◄ Plant cells—
a cross section
of a root

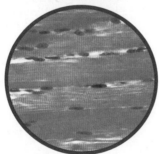

◄ Animal cells—
skeletal muscle

Comparing Plant and Animal Cells

Plant Cell

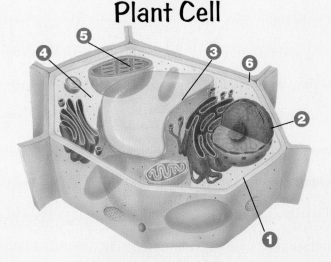

Animal Cell

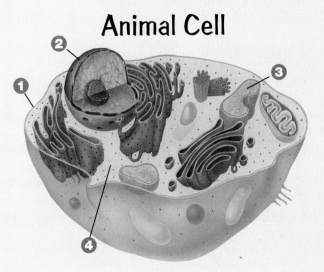

① **CELL MEMBRANE** A thin layer that surrounds all cells, the **cell membrane** allows water and dissolved materials to pass into and out of the cell.

② **NUCLEUS** (noo′klē əs) The **nucleus** controls all the cell's activities and is very important in cell reproduction.

③ **VACUOLE** (vak′yoo ōl) A **vacuole** is a large storage area filled with a liquid that contains various substances.

④ **CYTOPLASM** (sīt′ō plaz əm) The jellylike substance that fills much of the cell; other cell structures are found in the **cytoplasm.**

⑤ **CHLOROPLAST** (klôr′ə plast) The structure in which food making occurs, the **chloroplast** contains the green-colored pigment chlorophyll.

⑥ **CELL WALL** The **cell wall** is the tough outer covering of a plant cell that gives it a rigid shape; it is made of cellulose.

INVESTIGATION 1 WRAP-UP

REVIEW

1. List at least three basic life processes. Give examples of how plants and animals carry out these processes.

2. Draw and label a picture of a typical plant cell.

CRITICAL THINKING

3. How can a nonliving thing be mistaken for a living thing? How can a living thing be mistaken for a nonliving thing? Give examples of each.

4. Make a table that compares a typical plant cell with a typical animal cell.

How Do the Parts of a Plant Help It Meet Its Needs?

How do you obtain nutrients? Your body needs food to function. You have breakfast, lunch, and dinner. Sometimes you munch a snack in between. How does a plant, such as a geranium, get nutrients? You will investigate the parts of a plant and find out which ones help a plant get what it needs.

Activity

Take It Apart

Seed plants, such as a geranium and a maple tree, have the same basic parts—roots, stems, and leaves. As they mature, these plants develop flowers, fruits, and seeds. Examine a seed plant and get to know its parts.

Procedure

1. With other members of your group, observe a potted plant. In your *Science Notebook*, list all the plant parts you can see. Infer what parts might be hidden from view.

2. Examine the leaves. Describe and record their shape. Compare the width of a leaf to its length. Describe the thickness, texture, and color of a leaf. Describe how the leaves are attached. Record your observations. Draw a leaf.

3. Observe the stem. Record whether the stem has branches. Note whether the main stem is stiff or flexible. Record your observations.

MATERIALS

- goggles
- potted plant
- hand lens
- metric ruler
- newspaper
- plastic knife
- cut flower
- *Science Notebook*

SAFETY

Wear goggles during this activity.

Step 2

4. Carefully hold the pot upside down over a newspaper. Tap the bottom of the pot gently until the plant and soil come out. If the soil is stuck to the pot, use a plastic knife to loosen it. You may remove some of the soil so that you can observe plant parts that were hidden. **Record** your observations.

5. Note whether your plant has a flower. If your plant doesn't have a flower, **examine** a cut flower. Use a hand lens to **observe** the structures in the center of the flower. **Record** your observations. **Draw** the flower, showing all of its structures.

Analyze and Conclude

1. What are the main parts of a flowering plant?

2. On your drawings of a leaf and a flower, **label** any parts that you can identify.

3. In what ways is your plant similar to a tree? On what do you base your conclusions?

4. If you have ever examined other plants, **compare** ways in which these plants were different from the plant you observed in this activity. How were they the same?

Technology
Link
CD-ROM

INVESTIGATE FURTHER!

Use the **Science Processor CD-ROM**, *Plants* (Investigation 1, Inside Plants) to find out more about the parts of plants. View a magnified stem and leaf and learn about the inner workings of these plant parts.

Step 4

Roots and Stems

Reading Focus How are roots and stems alike and different?

Roots

Did you know that when you sit under a shady tree on a hot summer day, you are seeing half the tree or less? For all of the tree that you see above ground, there is an equal or even greater part below ground—the roots.

The **roots** are the underground foundation of a plant. Roots anchor the plant and absorb water and minerals. Roots also help transport these materials to other parts of the plant. Some roots, such as those of a carrot and a beet, also store food.

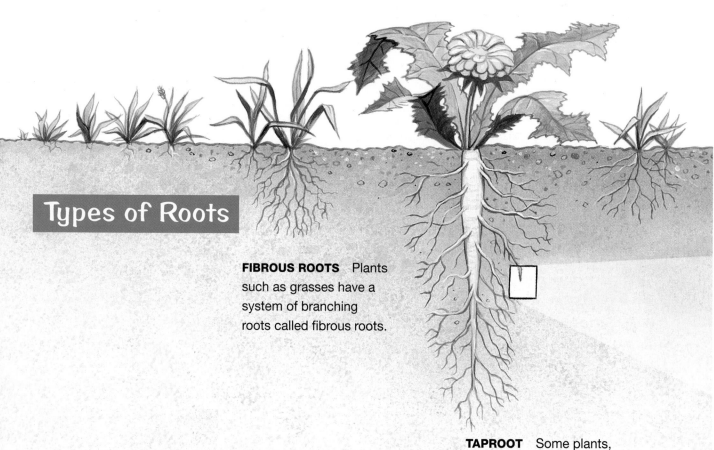

Types of Roots

FIBROUS ROOTS Plants such as grasses have a system of branching roots called fibrous roots.

TAPROOT Some plants, such as a carrot or a dandelion, have one main root, or taproot, that stores food.

Some plants have one main root, called a taproot. Other plants have many, branching roots, called fibrous roots. Compare these two types of roots in the drawing on page A16.

Study the drawing that shows the inside of a root. What type of tissue carries water toward the stem? What type of tissue carries nutrients from the leaves and stem into the root? What other kinds of tissue are found in a root? The root hairs near the tip of a root are very important. Water and minerals enter the root through these tiny structures. The drawing at the right shows how water and minerals move from the root hairs into the root's main transport system. Roots are observed in the activity on pages A14 and A15.

TRANSPORT IN A ROOT The arrows show the paths of water and minerals into a root. ▼

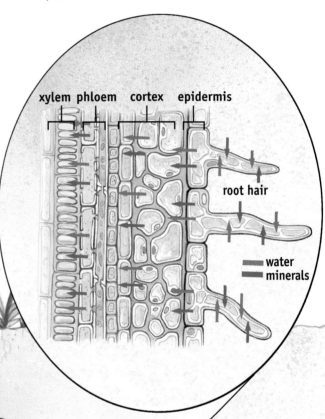

xylem phloem cortex epidermis

root hair

water
minerals

Inside a Root

CORTEX This layer connects the epidermis with the inner core.

XYLEM TISSUE This tissue is made of tubes that carry water and minerals from the soil upward.

EPIDERMIS This layer of cells covers the root.

PHLOEM TISSUE This tissue is made of tubes that carry sugars and other nutrients from the leaves through the stem and down to the root.

ROOT HAIRS These are tiny extensions that take in water and minerals.

ROOT CAP The tip of the root, called the root cap, pushes the root through the soil.

A17

Stems

The root is connected to the next main part of the plant—the stem. The **stem** is the part of a plant that connects the roots and the leaves. The stem supports the other above-ground parts of the plant, the leaves and flowers. The transport tissues that you saw in the roots on page A17 continue through the stem and into the leaves and flowers. Water and minerals move through the xylem tissue toward the leaves.

Sugar, the food made by the plant, moves through the phloem tissue toward the roots.

Stems vary in structure. Small flowering plants, such as buttercups and daisies, have short, thin, some-what soft stems. The trunks of large trees, such as oaks and maples, are hard, sturdy, and may be more than 30 m (100 ft) in height! Compare the nonwoody and woody stems in the drawings on this page. ■

CUTAWAY VIEW OF NONWOODY PLANT STEM This stem has thick walls and fibers running through it. The fibers give the stem its strength. This view shows the xylem and phloem cells that make up the transport system of the stem. Daisies and dandelions have nonwoody stems.

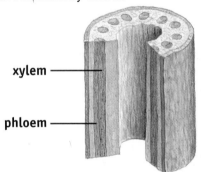

xylem

phloem

CUTAWAY VIEW OF WOODY PLANT STEM This trunk, which is actually a woody stem, is formed of many layers of cells. These layers have an outside protective covering called bark. This view shows the transport system of xylem and phloem. Each year the xylem cells form new layers of growth called annual rings.

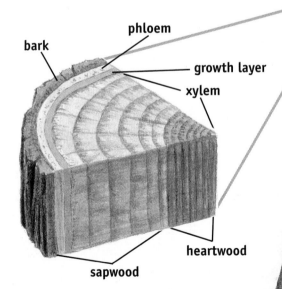

phloem

bark

growth layer

xylem

heartwood

sapwood

Using Math *A count of the number of annual rings can be used to estimate the age of a tree. About how old would you estimate this tree to be?*

Leaves

Reading Focus What are the parts of a leaf, and what is the function of each?

In autumn in some parts of the country, you will find great numbers of fallen red, yellow, and brown leaves. Why do plants have so many leaves? What do leaves do?

Look at the picture below of two kinds of leaves. A **leaf** is a plant part that grows out of the stem and is the food-making factory of a plant. The thin flat part of a leaf is called the blade. The blades of broad-leaved plants are often shaped so that the greatest amount of leaf is exposed to the Sun. Sunlight is an essential part of **photosynthesis** (fōt ō sin′thə sis), the food-making process in plants. The leaves of

Types of Leaves

NEEDLE LEAVES Plants such as a pine, a spruce, and a fir have needle leaves. The shape of these leaves helps reduce water loss.

BROAD LEAF Plants such as a maple and an oak are called broad-leaved trees and have broad flat leaves.

VEINS Along with the petiole, the veins form the transport system of the leaf. Water enters the leaf through the veins.

BLADE The blade is the broad flat part of a leaf.

PETIOLE The petiole is an extension of the xylem and phloem tubes of the stem.

Structure of a Leaf

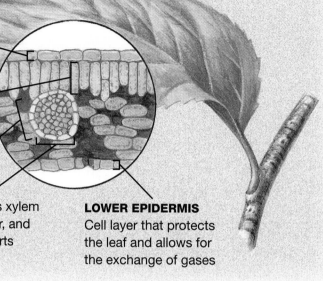

UPPER EPIDERMIS Cell layer that protects the leaf from drying out

PALISADE LAYER Columnlike cells where food making occurs

SPONGY LAYER Loosely-packed cells where food making occurs and where veins are located

VEIN Structure that contains xylem tissue, which transports water, and phloem tissue, which transports sugar and other nutrients

LOWER EPIDERMIS Cell layer that protects the leaf and allows for the exchange of gases

both broad-leaved plants and needle-leaved plants, such as a pine and a spruce, carry on this process.

Inside a Leaf

A typical leaf may be very thin, but it contains many cells, as shown above. If you cut across a leaf, producing a cross section, you'll find several layers of cells. The leaf's main function is to produce food for the plant. The structure of a leaf is well suited to that purpose.

Photosynthesis takes place in the two middle layers of cells. The top and bottom layers protect the leaf and keep it from drying out. Openings in the bottom layer allow for the exchange of gases with the environment. A leaf also contains many veins, which help transport water and manufactured food. ■

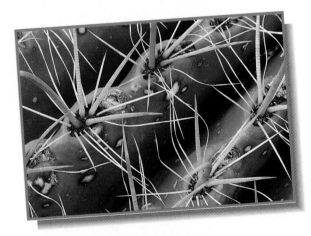

▲ The pointy spines of a cactus do not make food. They protect the stem from animal intruders. Cactus spines are modified leaves.

▲ In pea plants some leaves function as tendrils. They twist around objects and support the plant.

Energy Traps

Reading Focus What is needed for photosynthesis to occur, and what does this process produce?

Imagine that you're walking home from school and you begin to feel hungry. It would be great if you could manufacture a tasty snack on the spot. But you can't, of course. Your body can't produce its own food. But plants can.

Making Food

Plants produce their own food by using light energy, carbon dioxide, and water. Plants can't move around to find these things. But they can trap light energy and collect the substances they need to make their own food.

Plants trap energy in their leaves. Some leaf cells contain hundreds of disklike parts called chloroplasts. Recall that chloroplasts are tiny cell structures that contain a green pigment called chlorophyll. This pigment collects light energy from the Sun. Chlorophyll works much like a solar panel, absorbing light energy, which is then stored as food energy.

Chlorophyll uses the Sun's light energy to change two substances, carbon dioxide and water, into food. Carbon dioxide is a gas found in air. It enters the plant through tiny holes usually found on the underside of the leaves. Water enters the plant through the roots. Recall that transport tissue carries water from the roots to the stems to the leaves.

The food produced by a plant is called glucose (glōō′kōs), a form of sugar. The process of using light energy to combine carbon dioxide and water to produce glucose is called photosynthesis. *Photo-* means "light," and *synthesis* means "joining together."

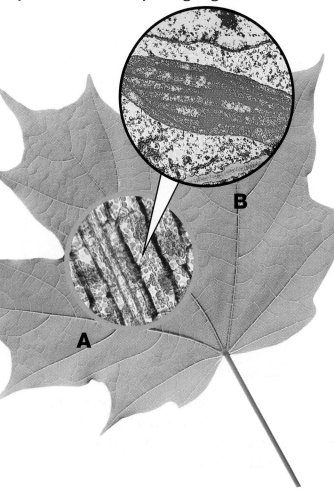

Chloroplasts are tiny green disklike cell parts that trap energy during photosynthesis.
(*A*) Groups of chloroplasts
(*B*) one enlarged chloroplast

Photosynthesis

Sun

light energy

carbon dioxide + water ➡️ glucose + oxygen

Plants trap light energy from the Sun during photosynthesis.

sunlight

■ Carbon dioxide enters the leaf through holes in its surface.

■ Oxygen, a waste product of photosynthesis, is released.

Glucose is produced in the leaf cells.

Water enters roots through root hairs at the tips of roots.

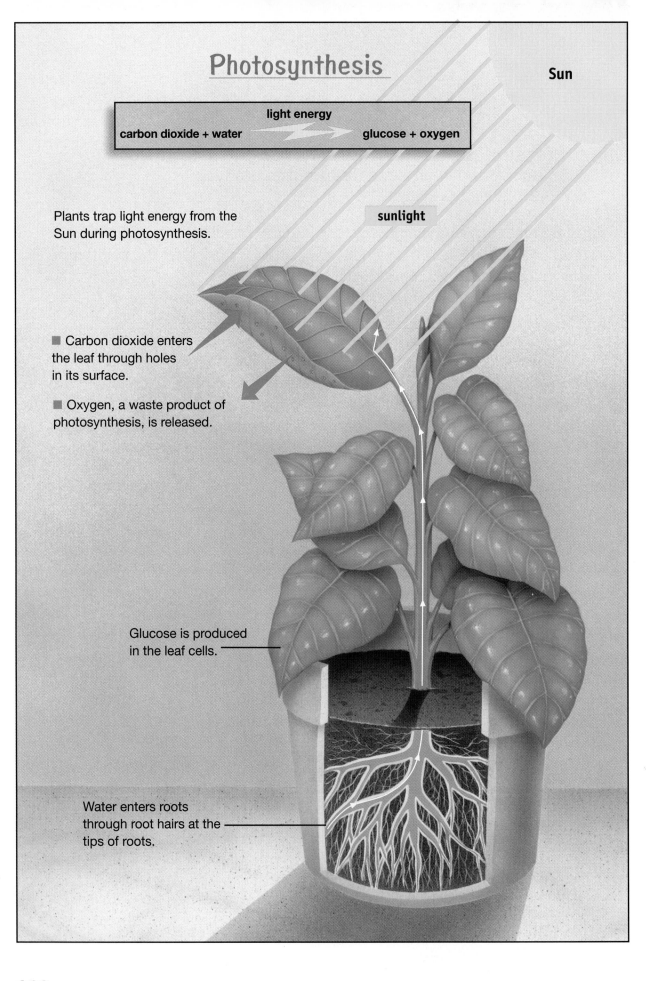

▲ **Radishes store starch in the roots.**

The drawing on page A22 shows the process by which plant cells produce glucose. In addition to glucose, photosynthesis produces a "waste" product. This waste product, oxygen, is one that humans and other animals need to survive. Oxygen and any leftover water leave the plant by way of the same tiny openings in the leaves through which carbon dioxide enters.

Storing and Using Food

Plants do not produce food all the time. Because photosynthesis requires sunlight, the process of trapping sunlight can't take place at night or on very

▼ **Lettuce stores starch in its leaves.**

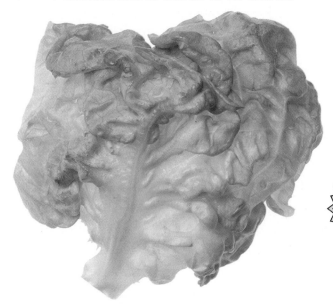

cloudy days. Although carbon dioxide is always available, water may be scarce at times. To survive, a plant must produce food when light energy, carbon dioxide, and water are all available. Many plants can store the food they make. Plants usually store food in the leaves, but sometimes they store it in the roots, stems, or other plant parts.

▲ **Celery stores starch in its leafstalks.**

Most plants store extra glucose in the form of starch, a chemical that is made up of a chain of simple sugars. This starch might be stored in the plant leaves (lettuce), in leafstalks (celery), in roots (carrots), or in underground stems (white potatoes).

Plants use the energy in glucose to grow, to produce seeds, and to carry out all their life functions. They use the energy from glucose in much the same way that you use the energy in the foods you eat. Both plant cells and animal cells use oxygen to release the energy in food. This process is called **cell respiration** (res pə rā′shən). ■

Internet Field Trip

Visit **www.eduplace.com** to find out more about the life processes of plants.

Plant Responses

Reading Focus What are some ways a plant responds to its environment?

Have you ever seen someone grow a sweet potato plant in a glass of water? If so, you probably noticed that the roots grow down into the glass. The stems grow up, usually toward a light source. The sweet potato plant is reacting, or responding, to its environment. A plant response to conditions in the environment is called a **tropism** (trō′piz əm).

Growth Toward Gravity

Roots respond to Earth's gravity by growing toward the center of Earth. Growing toward the center of Earth is a geotropic response. The word *tropism* comes from a Greek word that means "a turning." The word part *geo-* means "Earth." So *geotropism* is a turning (of the roots) toward Earth. This growth response ensures that the roots will grow down into the soil, the plant's source of water and nutrients. Leaves and stems have the opposite response to gravity. They grow away from Earth's center. This response helps ensure that leaves and stems will be exposed to sunlight, which the plant needs to make its food.

Growth Toward Light

Leaves and stems grow toward a source of light. Growing toward light is a phototropic response. *Photo-* means "light." You have probably seen the leaves of houseplants turned toward a bright light source. Stems may also bend toward that light source. The bending of stems occurs because they are actually growing toward light. Such growth allows the leaves to capture the greatest amount of light, which is needed for the process of photosynthesis. What can you do with a houseplant to keep the stems and leaves from bending in one direction?

Growth Toward Water

When plant roots are in soil that has lots of water in one area, they grow toward the wet area. This kind of growth is a hydrotropic response. (*Hydro-* means "water.") However, roots do not "know" where the moisture is. They do not "try" to find the water. Instead, when roots come into contact with moist soil, they continue to grow toward the moisture. Roots touching only very dry soil may grow very slowly or not at all.

Hanging On

Some plants have threadlike parts called tendrils that wrap around objects to support the plant. This response is another kind of tropism called thigmotropism, or response to touch. (*Thigmo-* means "touch.") Picture 4 on page A25 shows the thigmotropic response of a pea plant.

① Roots showing a geotropic response. ② Leaves showing a phototropic response.
③ Two plants showing a hydrotropic response. ④ Tendrils curling around garden stakes, showing a thigmotropic response.

INVESTIGATION 2 WRAP-UP

REVIEW

1. Draw a leaf, such as a maple leaf, and label the veins, blade, and petiole.

2. Describe the roles of xylem tissue and phloem tissue in stems.

CRITICAL THINKING

3. Explain why the parts of the word *photosynthesis (photo-* and *synthesis)* help explain the process of photosynthesis.

4. What do you think would happen to the roots of a plant if you turned the plant upside down for two weeks? Explain.

INVESTIGATION 3

HOW DO THE PARTS OF AN ANIMAL HELP IT MEET ITS NEEDS?

Roots, stems, and leaves help a plant meet its needs. Animals have body parts, too. These parts appear very different from those found in plants. But surprisingly, an animal's body parts have the same basic job as a plant's parts—to help the organism meet its needs.

Activity

Come and Get It

You know that a plant's roots absorb water. And you've learned that carbon dioxide is taken in through its leaves. A plant uses these materials to make food. Unlike plants, animals must obtain food from their environment. Find out what body parts help a snail do this.

MATERIALS
- goggles
- plastic gloves
- garden snail
- plastic container
- hand lens
- snail food
- *Science Notebook*

SAFETY
Wear goggles and plastic gloves while doing this activity.

Procedure

1. Obtain a garden snail from your teacher. Place the snail on the inside wall of a plastic container.

2. Use a hand lens to observe the snail. In your *Science Notebook*, make a sketch of the snail. Label any body parts that you can identify.

Step 2

3. List each body part that you labeled. Infer the job done by each part listed. Record your inferences.

4. Add food to the plastic container and place the snail near the food. Observe the snail's behavior. Record your observations.

5. Identify any body parts that you think help the snail obtain food. Describe these body parts.

6. Compare your observations with those of another group of students in your class.

Analyze and Conclude

1. Make a chart that compares the basic needs of a snail with those of a plant. List any similarities.

2. Compare the way that a snail obtains food with the way a plant obtains food.

3. Both a snail and a plant use food. Hypothesize whether the food is used for the same purpose in both organisms. Explain your reasoning.

UNIT PROJECT LINK

For this Unit Project you will create a museum display comparing systems in a plant, an invertebrate, and a vertebrate. Research where each organism lives and what it eats. Write a brief report as part of your display.

Technology Link

For more help with your Unit Project, go to **www.eduplace.com**.

Science in Literature

STOP THE DISAPPEARING ACT

"Follow the trunks of the trees as they rise straight up from the forest floor. You'll see them open like umbrellas, branching out to form the rooflike canopy of the rain forest. In this dense layer of green, leaves bathed in full sunlight absorb energy and use it to make food."

Why Save the Rain Forest?
by Donald Silver
Illustrated by Patricia J. Wynne
Julian Messner, 1993

Read about the role of rain forest trees in keeping carbon dioxide from building up in the air. In *Why Save the Rain Forest?* Donald Silver describes the importance of photosynthesis in balancing the life-support systems of Earth.

Staying Alive!

Reading Focus What life processes do all living things carry out?

A Look Back

You've compared the structure of plant cells and animal cells. You learned that plants obtain and use materials from their environment. You also learned that through the process of photosynthesis, plants are able to produce their own food.

You've seen how plant organs—roots, stems, and leaves — help plants meet their needs. Animals must also meet their needs. Like plants, they have organs and systems that help meet those needs. Let's take a look at the organ systems of two animals—the frog and the human.

Frogs and Plants—Alike or Not?

Like a plant, a frog carries out basic life processes. The frog obtains and digests food. Digestion is the process of breaking down food into nutrients that cells can absorb. The digested food provides the frog with the energy needed to carry out its life processes. The nutrients in food are also used to build new cells and to repair damaged cells. A plant uses food in these same ways.

As it carries out its life processes, a frog produces waste products, which are removed from the body. Plants also produce and release waste products as they carry out their life processes.

Organ Systems of a Frog

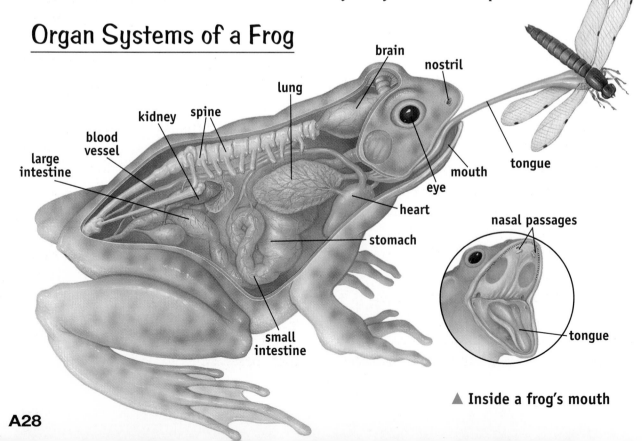

brain
nostril
lung
kidney
spine
blood vessel
large intestine
mouth
tongue
eye
heart
stomach
small intestine
nasal passages
tongue

▲ Inside a frog's mouth

Food Getting and Digesting

A major difference between a frog and a plant involves the way each obtains food. In the presence of light, plants take in water and carbon dioxide and make sugar, which is their food. They give off oxygen as a waste product of the food-making process. All animals, including frogs, must obtain their food from their surroundings. They must then digest, or break down, the food to release the energy it contains.

A frog has a group of organs, the digestive system, that work together to digest food. As you read, find parts of the frog's digestive system in the drawing on page A28.

A frog's digestive system begins at its mouth. A frog uses its tongue to obtain food. Notice from the drawing that a frog's tongue is attached to the front of its mouth. By flicking out its sticky tongue, a frog can catch passing insects.

Next, the frog swallows the insect whole, without chewing. Frogs have very tiny teeth that are good for gripping, not biting or chewing! The food is pushed down the frog's throat in an interesting way. As the frog blinks, its large eyeballs push the insect down its throat!

The mouth connects to a short tube, the esophagus (i säf'ə gəs), that connects to the stomach. Partly digested food remains a short time in the stomach and then moves on to the coiled small intestine. Digestion continues in this organ.

Digested food containing nutrients is absorbed from the small intestine into the bloodstream. The bloodstream carries the nutrients to all the frog's cells. The small intestine joins to a large intestine, which narrows to a rectum. Undigested food leaves the body through an opening at the end of the rectum.

Gas Exchange

The cells of a frog's body use oxygen to break down sugar obtained from food. Oxygen is brought into a frog's body by its respiratory system. Air, which contains oxygen, passes through a frog's mouth and down a tube to the lungs. Here, oxygen is picked up by the frog's transport system. At the same time, the transport system picks up carbon dioxide, a waste gas. The carbon dioxide is carried from the blood to the lungs and is then exhaled, or breathed out.

Transporting and Excreting

The circulatory system is the frog's transport system. A frog's circulatory system includes a heart that pumps the blood through blood vessels to all parts of the frog's body. Blood carries oxygen and digested food to the body's cells.

As the frog carries on its life processes, its cells produce waste products. If allowed to build up, these wastes become harmful. Wastes are removed, or excreted, from the frog's body by the excretory (eks'krə tôr ē) and digestive systems.

Blood traveling through the body carries carbon dioxide and other wastes from cells. Blood passes through the kidneys, which are organs of the excretory system that filter the blood. The kidneys remove wastes, minerals, and excess water from the frog's blood. The liquid wastes are stored in a bladder and then passed out of the body.

Human Body Systems

You've just learned about what's inside a frog. What would you find inside a human body? The same life processes that keep a frog alive also keep a human being alive. People must digest food and get rid of the waste products of digestion. They must breathe in air and release the waste products of respiration. They must also circulate the nutrients that are made available during digestion.

The drawings on this page show four human body systems. On the left is a drawing of the digestive and excretory systems. On the right is a drawing of the circulatory and respiratory systems. You can probably recognize some of the organs in these four systems. For example, find the stomach, kidneys, lungs, and heart.

In the next two chapters, you'll learn in more detail how human body systems work to keep the body alive and well.

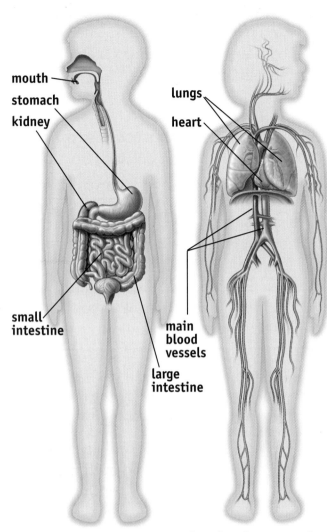

mouth
stomach
kidney
small intestine
lungs
heart
main blood vessels
large intestine

▲ The digestive and excretory systems

▲ The circulatory and respiratory systems

INVESTIGATION 3 WRAP-UP

THINK IT WRITE IT

REVIEW

1. Describe the major difference in food-getting between plants and animals.

2. Why is it vital for living things such as frogs to digest food?

CRITICAL THINKING

3. How is the transport system of a plant similar to the transport system of a frog? How do the systems differ?

4. Explain how the digestive and circulatory systems work together to supply nutrients and energy to the body's cells. Use information about the frog to support your answer.

REFLECT & EVALUATE

Word Power

Write the letter of the term that best matches the definition. *Not all terms will be used.*

a. chloroplast
b. cytoplasm
c. life processes
d. nucleus
e. organ
f. photosynthesis
g. tropisms
h. vacuole

1. Cell structure that controls all the cell's activities
2. Plant responses to conditions in the environment
3. Functions that a living thing must carry out to stay alive
4. Jellylike substance that fills most of a cell
5. Food-making process in plants
6. Chlorophyll-containing structure in a plant cell

Check What You Know

Write the word in each pair that correctly completes each sentence.

1. Tubes that carry nutrients from the leaves through the stem and down to the roots are (xylem, phloem) tissue.
2. The process by which animal cells and plant cells use oxygen to release energy in foods is (photosynthesis, cell respiration).
3. The outermost layer of an animal cell is the (cell membrane, cell wall).

Problem Solving

1. A potted plant is growing on a windowsill in bright light. The plant is rotated one-half turn each morning. How would this turning affect the way the plant's stems grow?

2. In your own words, explain why a leaf can be called an "energy trap."

3. Explain the function of digestion; use digestion in a frog to support your explanation.

Make a sketch of this plant cell. Label the parts. In a short paragraph describe how the parts in a drawing of an animal cell would be different from the parts in a drawing of a plant cell.

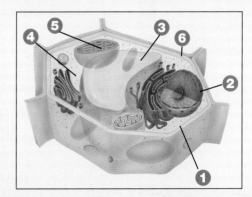

CHAPTER 2

DIGESTION AND RESPIRATION

Human body systems consist of many organs working together. What happens to the food that we eat? What is the purpose of breathing? In this chapter you'll explore the workings of two important body systems—the digestive system and the respiratory system.

Connecting to Science

CULTURE

Ancient Remedies Treatment for problems of the digestive system dates back to ancient times. As long ago as 2500 B.C. the Chinese treated various digestive disorders with acupuncture. Acupuncture is a treatment in which very thin needles are placed into the body at key points. This treatment has been proven to control appetite and to reduce stomach upset.

The ancient Chinese also used plants to treat digestive disorders. Plants used in this way are called herbs. The yellow underground stem of Chinese rhubarb has been used for more than 2,000 years to regulate digestion. Another herb used as medicine since ancient times is garlic. The Chinese, Babylonians, Greeks, Romans, Hindus, and Egyptians all used garlic to treat various intestinal disorders. Read on to learn more about the human digestive system.

Coming Up

INVESTIGATION 1

HOW DOES THE DIGESTIVE SYSTEM WORK?
.... A34

INVESTIGATION 2

HOW DOES THE RESPIRATORY SYSTEM WORK?
.... A44

◄ Dr. Malcolm Johnson in front of a chart of acupuncture points

INVESTIGATION ①

HOW DOES THE DIGESTIVE SYSTEM WORK?

Did you ever swallow a large piece of food without properly chewing it? How did that feel? For food to be used by your body, it must be broken down by the digestive system. The breakdown begins in the mouth.

Activity

Sink Your Teeth Into This

Have you ever looked very carefully at your teeth? Are they all the same size and shape? Are the edges of your teeth smooth or ragged? Find out in this activity.

MATERIALS
- mirror
- celery stick
- *Science Notebook*

SAFETY //////
During this activity, eat foods only with your teacher's permission.

Procedure

1. Use a mirror to **observe** your teeth. Count the number of teeth in your lower jaw. Then count the number of teeth in your upper jaw. **Record** these numbers in your *Science Notebook*. **Compare** the numbers with those of other students in your class.

2. Look for four main kinds of teeth in your mouth. Look at the drawing to the right, which shows the teeth in a person's mouth. In your *Science Notebook*, **list** the four kinds and describe how they are alike and how they are different.

Step 2

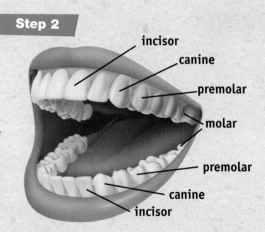

incisor
canine
premolar
molar
premolar
canine
incisor

3. Talk with group members about how the four kinds of teeth differ. Infer why these teeth are different.

4. Close your teeth and observe how the upper teeth and lower teeth meet. In your *Science Notebook,* describe how your teeth meet. Note whether the way the teeth meet affects how you chew your food.

5. Eat a celery stick. Note which teeth you use to bite the celery. Note which teeth you use to chew the celery. Record this information in your *Science Notebook.*

Analyze and Conclude

1. How many teeth do most students have in their lower jaw? in their upper jaw? Is there a difference between the kinds of teeth in the upper jaw and the lower jaw?

2. In what ways do you use your front teeth? In what ways do you use your back teeth? How do the shapes of the front teeth and the back teeth differ? Describe how the shape of your teeth is related to how you use them.

INVESTIGATE FURTHER!

RESEARCH

Find pictures of the teeth of different animals such as a squirrel, a deer, a bear, an alligator, and a wolf. Compare the shapes and sizes of the teeth. Find out the diet of each animal. Hypothesize whether diet and tooth shape are related.

Science in Literature

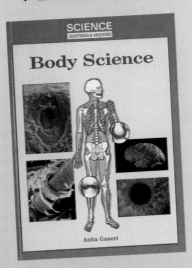

SCIENCE
QUESTIONS & ANSWERS

Body Science

Anita Ganeri

Body Science
by Anita Ganeri
Dillon Press, 1992

WHEN FOOD GOES DOWN THE "WRONG WAY"

"When you swallow a piece of food, a flap called the epiglottis covers the top of your windpipe, and the food goes down your esophagus and into your digestive system. But this process can go wrong. If you accidentally breathe in as you swallow the food, the epiglottis opens up. Then the food gets into your windpipe. You may choke on it. . . ."

Does your food ever go down the "wrong way"? Does your stomach ever rumble? Find out about your digestive system and many other parts of the human body as you read *Body Science* by Anita Ganeri.

Activity

How Sweet It Is

Some foods contain sugar. You'll use a glucose test strip to find out if glucose, a kind of sugar, is present in certain foods. You'll also find out how a chemical called an enzyme (en'zīm) *can change a sugar from one form to another.*

MATERIALS
- goggles
- marker
- four paper cups (3 oz)
- dropper
- apple juice
- orange juice
- cranberry juice
- milk
- glucose test strips
- lactase drops
- *Science Notebook*

SAFETY

Wear goggles while doing this activity.

Procedure

1. Use a marker to label four paper cups *apple juice*, *orange juice*, *cranberry juice*, and *milk*.

2. Use a dropper to add ten drops of apple juice to the first paper cup. Wash the dropper thoroughly. Then add ten drops of orange juice to the second paper cup.

3. Wash the dropper. Add ten drops of cranberry juice to the third cup. Wash the dropper again. Add ten drops of milk to the fourth cup.

4. You will use a glucose test strip to find out if the liquid in each cup contains the sugar glucose. A glucose test strip changes from light green to dark green or brown when it contacts glucose. In your *Science Notebook*, **make a chart** like the one shown below. **Predict** what will happen to the test strip when each liquid is tested. **Record** your predictions in your chart.

Glucose Present?		
Food	**Prediction**	**Result**
apple juice		

See **SCIENCE** and **MATH TOOLBOX** page H11 if you need to review **Making a Chart to Organize Data.**

5. Test each liquid by dipping a dry glucose test strip into each cup. **Record** your results in your chart.

6. Lactose is a kind of sugar found in milk. Lactase is a chemical, called an enzyme, made by the body. Lactase breaks down lactose to simple sugars, such as glucose. Put one drop of lactase into the cup of milk. Now dip a dry glucose test strip into the milk. **Record** your observations.

Analyze and Conclude

1. What happened to the glucose test strip in the apple juice, orange juice, cranberry juice, and milk? Which liquid contained glucose? How do you know?

2. Compare the two glucose test strips you used in the milk both before and after you added the lactase. How were they alike or different? **Infer** what could have caused a difference in the results.

3. Recall that lactase breaks down lactose, the sugar in milk. Some people do not make enough lactase. If such people drink milk or milk products, they can become ill. **Hypothesize** how these people might be able to drink milk without becoming ill.

Step 5

MILK

UNIT PROJECT LINK

For the plant that you selected for your museum display, research the plant system that allows for gas exchange. For the two animals you chose, research the respiratory system of each. Create a display that compares all three systems. Your display might include posters, models, or another medium of your choice.

 **Technology**Link

For more help with your Unit Project, go to **www.eduplace.com**.

How Digestion Starts

Reading Focus How is food digested as it moves from the mouth to the stomach?

Your Stomach "Speaks"

Your body sends you signals when it is time to eat. Many people feel tired, weak, or even grouchy when they're hungry. Yet it isn't really food the body needs. The body's cells need chemicals called nutrients (noo′trē ənts) for energy, to build new cells, to repair damaged cells, and to control body processes.

Foods provide tasty packaging for nutrients. After you take a bite, food travels through about 9 m (30 ft) of digestive organs. These organs make up the human **digestive system**, in which food is broken down into a form that body cells can use.

From Your Plate to a Cell

The digestive organs grind, mash, and churn food into smaller and smaller particles. They also release chemicals that soften food and change it from one form to another. Once food has been changed to a form that cells can use, it passes out of the digestive system. The nutrients from food pass into the bloodstream and then to the body's cells.

Digestion in the Mouth

Think about your last meal. The digestive process probably began before you took your first bite. At just the sight and smell of the food, your salivary (sal′ə ver ē) glands went to work.

The drawing at the bottom of page A39 shows your salivary glands, which are located under your tongue and near your ears. The glands produce **saliva** (sə lī′və), the watery liquid that moistens the mouth and food. Each day as much as $1\frac{1}{2}$ L (about 6 c) of saliva flow into your mouth. Saliva begins the chemical breakdown of the food.

The Role of the Teeth

When you eat solid food, you bite off pieces with your front teeth, the incisors (in sī′zərz). The incisors are cutting teeth as the activity on pages A34 and A35 shows. The teeth on either side of them are canines, which tear food. To help the digestive process, you chew your food well with your back grinding teeth, the premolars and molars.

From about 6 months to 26 months of age, your baby teeth grow in. Then those teeth fall out and are replaced by permanent teeth. All your permanent teeth will appear by age 20. Look at the drawing of teeth on page A39 and find the four main kinds of teeth. The cutting, tearing, and grinding action of the teeth physically breaks food into smaller pieces, helping digestion.

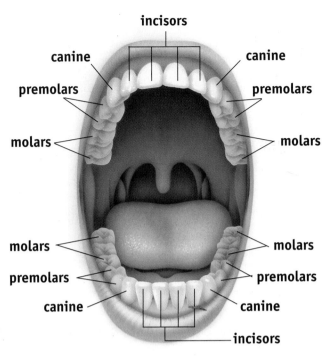

▲ Teeth in an adult's mouth

Your teeth would not work very well without your tongue. The tongue is the muscular organ that helps you swallow and pushes food against your teeth. After you bite, slice, and tear food, your tongue pushes it to the grinding surfaces of the back teeth.

As you chew, your salivary glands produce chemicals called **enzymes** (en'zīmz), which help break down food. Ptyalin (tī'ə lin) is an enzyme in saliva that breaks starch into simple sugars. After food is ground and mixed with saliva, it becomes a soft, wet mass. This mass of food is ready to be swallowed.

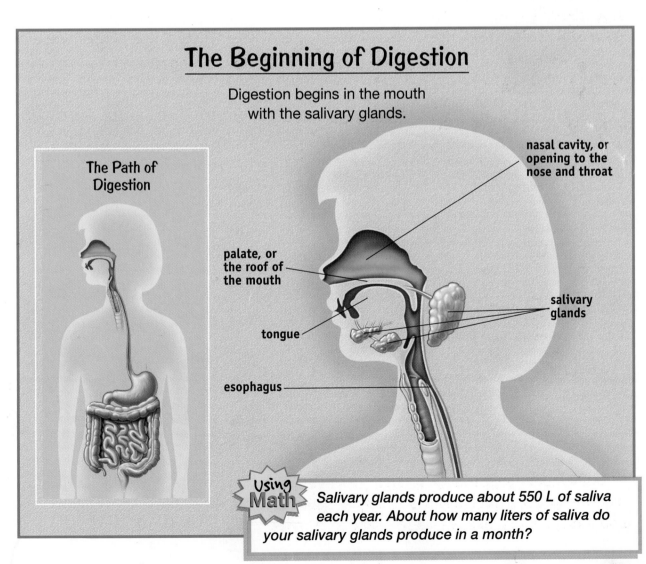

The Beginning of Digestion

Digestion begins in the mouth with the salivary glands.

The Path of Digestion

nasal cavity, or opening to the nose and throat

palate, or the roof of the mouth

salivary glands

tongue

esophagus

Using Math *Salivary glands produce about 550 L of saliva each year. About how many liters of saliva do your salivary glands produce in a month?*

A39

Swallowing

You control the start of a swallow. When the food is moist and soft, your tongue pushes it to the back of the throat. Once food reaches the back of the throat, automatic processes take over. Then the food cannot go down the "wrong pipe"—the trachea, or windpipe.

Look at the numbers in the drawings below to see what happens during the automatic part of swallowing.

Choking

Sometimes the automatic processes of digestion fail. Suppose you talk and laugh while eating. The food in your mouth can enter the nose or the windpipe. You can even choke. A person trained in giving the Heimlich maneuver (hīm′lik mə noo′vər) can help to dislodge the stuck food. First, the trained person wraps his arms around the choking person under that person's ribs.

Stages of Swallowing

1 The tongue pushes food to the back of the throat.

2 The back part of the palate (pal′ət) rises up to close the opening to the nose. (This keeps food from backing up into the nose.)

3 A flap of tissue closes the trachea, keeping food from entering it.

4 Throat muscles squeeze food to the top of the esophagus (i säf′ə gəs). The **esophagus** is the muscular tube that connects the mouth to the stomach.

5 The palate lowers, opening the passage to the nose.

6 The flap of tissue to the windpipe rises.

7 Food is now safely in the esophagus.

8 Food will continue moving toward the stomach.

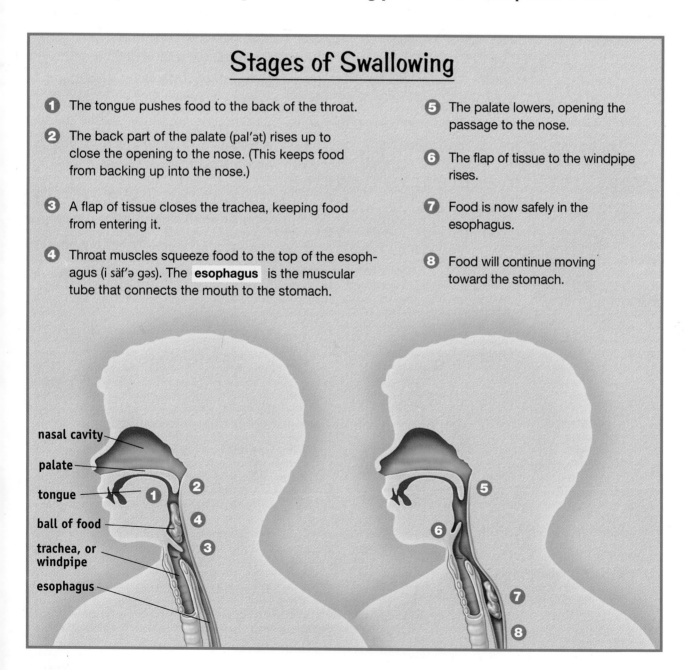

nasal cavity

palate

tongue

ball of food

trachea, or windpipe

esophagus

Then he presses strongly in and up under the breastbone. This action can help to force the stuck food up and out of the windpipe.

Down to the Stomach

The esophagus moves food along, using a wavelike motion known as **peristalsis** (per ə stal′sis). Rings of muscles contract, or tighten, above the mass of food. At the same time, rings of muscles below the food relax. This contracting and relaxing of muscles pushes the food down to the stomach.

The esophagus ends at the **stomach**, a muscular organ that stores food and helps digest it. Between the esophagus and the stomach is a round muscle that acts as a gatekeeper. This muscle opens, allowing the swallowed food into the stomach. Once the food is in the stomach, the muscle closes, preventing the food from moving back into the esophagus.

In the Stomach

An adult's stomach can hold about 1 L (1 qt) of food. The food stays in the stomach two to six hours, where it is further broken down.

Even before food reaches the stomach, glands in the stomach lining begin to produce digestive juices. One juice, hydrochloric acid, is strong enough to make a hole in a carpet or dissolve metal. Why, then, isn't the stomach digested by its own acid? The walls of the stomach and other digestive organs are protected. They produce mucus (myoo′kəs), a slippery material that forms a thick, protective coating inside digestive organs.

The stomach also makes digestive enzymes. Some stomach enzymes begin to break down the proteins found in meat, eggs, dairy products, and beans. Like the esophagus, the stomach undergoes peristalsis. Waves of muscle action mash and churn the food and digestive juices. The food soon becomes a thick, soupy liquid called chyme (kīm). Then it is ready to leave the stomach.

Two to six hours after food is swallowed, chyme begins to leave the stomach. Sugars and starches leave first, then proteins. Fats remain in the stomach longest. A few simple chemicals, such as sugar, alcohol, and some medicines, pass directly from the stomach to the bloodstream. But most nutrients are passed along for further digestion. ■

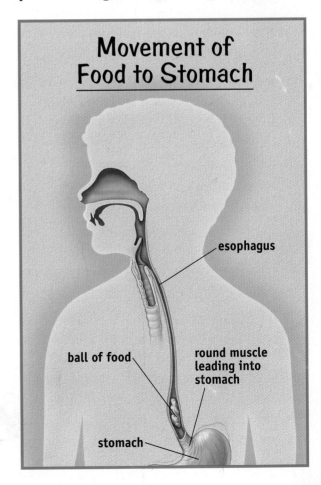

Movement of Food to Stomach

esophagus

ball of food

round muscle leading into stomach

stomach

How Digestion Ends

> **Reading Focus** What happens to food after it leaves the stomach?

Digestion in the Small Intestine

Did you know that a person can live without a stomach? How can this be? Look at the drawing. Recall that the main role of the stomach is to store food, not digest it. Most nutrients are absorbed into the bloodstream in the next part of the digestive system—the small intestine. The **small intestine** is the long, coiled organ where most digestion takes place.

The "small" intestine is not really small. About 6 m (20 ft) long, it can be three times as long as the body it occupies. You can see that it is coiled, allowing it to fit inside the body. It is called the *small* intestine because it is narrower than the *large* intestine.

Recall that in the stomach, food becomes a soupy liquid called chyme. Chyme from the stomach enters the first part of the small intestine. Then, over the next five hours, the digestive process is completed. The small intestine produces digestive juices and enzymes, such as the enzyme lactase. As the activity on pages A36 and A37 shows, lactase changes lactose, a sugar found in milk, to glucose, a simpler form of sugar.

Other organs work with the small intestine. Find the liver in the drawing. The liver is an organ that performs more than 500 functions in several body systems. One function in digestion is to produce bile, which breaks fats into smaller pieces.

Made in the liver, bile is stored in the gallbladder, a small pear-shaped organ. The gallbladder supplies bile to the small intestine as it is needed. Another organ, the pancreas, lies behind the stomach and is connected to the small intestine.

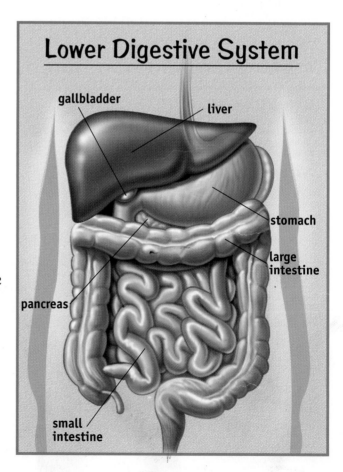

Lower Digestive System

gallbladder

liver

stomach

large intestine

pancreas

small intestine

The pancreas produces pancreatic juices. These juices are a mixture of digestive enzymes and other substances that aid in digestion.

Absorption in the Small Intestine

Most carbohydrates, proteins, and water are absorbed in the second part of the small intestine. Vitamins and minerals that dissolve in water are also absorbed there.

In the wall of the small intestine are **villi** (vil′ī), shown below. Villi are like the loops on a terry-cloth towel. In the villi is a network of blood vessels. Dissolved nutrients pass from the small intestine through these vessels into the blood. The blood then carries the nutrients to every cell in the body.

Waste Removal

After food passes through the small intestine, some material, such as fiber, still remains undigested. Fiber is important to digestion. It helps in the movement of food through the digestive system. But humans cannot digest fiber. It must be passed out of the body.

Peristalsis moves undigested matter into the large intestine. The **large intestine** is the organ that absorbs water and salts from undigested material. It returns much of the water through its walls to the bloodstream. The large intestine also moves undigested material out of the body. About 24 to 48 hours after a meal is eaten, the undigested materials pass out of the body through an opening called the anus (ā′nəs). ■

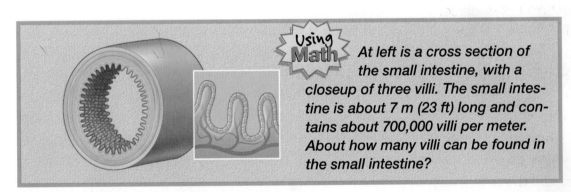

Using Math

At left is a cross section of the small intestine, with a closeup of three villi. The small intestine is about 7 m (23 ft) long and contains about 700,000 villi per meter. About how many villi can be found in the small intestine?

INVESTIGATION 1 WRAP-UP

THINK IT WRITE IT

REVIEW

1. What is the function of the digestive system? Describe digestion in the mouth and the stomach.

2. Explain why a person can live without a stomach.

CRITICAL THINKING

3. As food moves through the digestive system, it is changed in two main ways. Identify these two changes. Explain the role of the mouth, stomach, small intestine, and large intestine in these changes.

4. Describe the structure of the small intestine. How does this structure aid in the absorption of nutrients?

INVESTIGATION 2

HOW DOES THE RESPIRATORY SYSTEM WORK?

Breathe in. Hold that air. Then breathe out. What is going on inside your body when you inhale and exhale? In this investigation you'll learn what is happening to air as it moves through your respiratory system.

Activity

Breathing Rates

Your breathing rate is how often you inhale in one minute. Find out what things affect this rate.

MATERIALS
- chair
- timer
- *Science Notebook*

Procedure

Sit in a chair in a relaxed position. Have a group member count the number of times you breathe in during one minute. Have another member use a timer to keep track of the time. Record the number in your *Science Notebook*.

Predict how exercise will affect your breathing rate. Record your prediction. Run in place for one minute. Then count and record how many times you breathe in during one minute.

Analyze and Conclude

1. How did exercise affect your breathing rate? Infer why exercise had this effect.

2. Hypothesize about other things that could affect your breathing rate. Explain your ideas.

Activity

Lung Power

Without special devices you can't look inside your chest to observe how your lungs work. But you can make a working model of a lung in this activity.

MATERIALS
- 2 balloons (1 small, 1 large)
- drinking straw
- tape
- scissors
- small clear plastic bottle with bottom cut off
- modeling clay
- *Science Notebook*

Procedure

1. Work with your group to build a model of a lung. Pull the opening of a small balloon over one end of a drinking straw. Use tape to attach the balloon to the straw.

2. Cut the neck off a large balloon. Have a group member hold a plastic bottle from which the bottom has been cut off. Stretch the balloon over the cut end of the bottle. Secure the balloon with tape.

3. Push the end of the straw with the small balloon into the mouth of the bottle. Then use modeling clay to seal the mouth of the bottle and to hold the straw in place.

4. Predict what will happen to the small balloon when you pull down and push up on the large balloon. Record your prediction in your *Science Notebook*.

5. Observe what happens when you pull down and then push up on the large balloon. Make drawings of your observations.

Step 3

Analyze and Conclude

1. What happened to the small balloon when you pulled down on the large balloon? What happened when you pushed up?

2. Based on observations of your model, hypothesize what happens in your body when you breathe.

3. You have just made a model of the way the lungs work. Describe at least one way in which this model differs from a real lung.

Breathing Basics

> **Reading Focus** What happens when you breathe in and breathe out?

Breathing is the process by which the body takes in "fresh" air containing oxygen and pushes out "used" air containing waste gases. The parts of the body that work together to take air into the body and push it back out form the **respiratory system**. The drawing below illustrates the parts of this system.

Air Enters

What happens when you take in a breath of air, or inhale? Air can enter through either the mouth or nose.

Your nose both warms and moistens the air you breathe. Small hairs inside the nose trap dust and other particles in the air. If tiny particles slip past the hairs, they are trapped by mucus. On page A41 you read about mucus in the digestive system. The respiratory system is also lined with a sticky layer of mucus.

From your mouth or nose, the inhaled air moves to the back of your throat. There it enters the trachea (trā′kē ə), or windpipe. The **trachea** is the air tube that connects the throat to the lungs. Find the trachea below.

To feel your trachea, gently move your hand up and down the front of your neck. You will feel bumpy rings of cartilage (kärt′′l ij), a tough but bendable material. Cartilage helps the trachea keep its shape. Without cartilage, the trachea would collapse when you inhale.

The Respiratory System

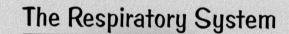

NOSE AND MOUTH The nose and mouth take in and let out air.

LUNGS The **lungs** are two spongy organs that expand when they fill with air.

TRACHEA The **trachea**, also called the windpipe, is the air passage connecting the throat to the lungs.

DIAPHRAGM The **diaphragm** (dī′ə fram) is a dome-shaped muscle that separates the chest from the stomach area.

Muscles Do the Work

The activity on page A45 shows that the breathing process starts in your chest. The process depends on the diaphragm and the muscles between your ribs. Follow the numbered steps in the drawing to see what happens during breathing.

Inhaling

1. When you begin to inhale, the rib muscles tighten and get shorter, pulling the chest out and up.

2. The diaphragm tightens and moves down, further increasing the space inside the chest.

3. When the space inside the chest increases, the lungs expand and air rushes in.

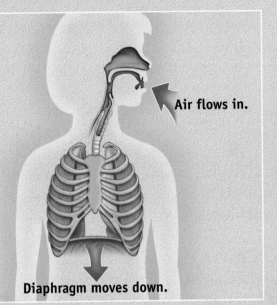

Air flows in.

Diaphragm moves down.

Exhaling

1. When you begin to exhale, the rib muscles relax and get longer and the chest gets smaller.

2. The diaphragm relaxes and moves up, making less space inside the chest.

3. Air is forced out of the lungs as the space in the chest gets smaller.

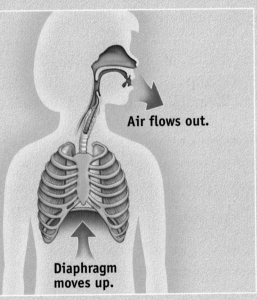

Air flows out.

Diaphragm moves up.

Breathless!

Your breathing rate is the number of times you inhale each minute. When you're sleeping or sitting quietly, your rate is slow. If you're walking, the rate increases, since your body needs a greater amount of oxygen supplied to the lungs. If you're exercising heavily, your breathing rate increases still more. The only way to get more oxygen into the body is to breathe more quickly and deeply. The activity on page A44 shows how a person's breathing rate increases during exercise. ∎

Exchanging Gases

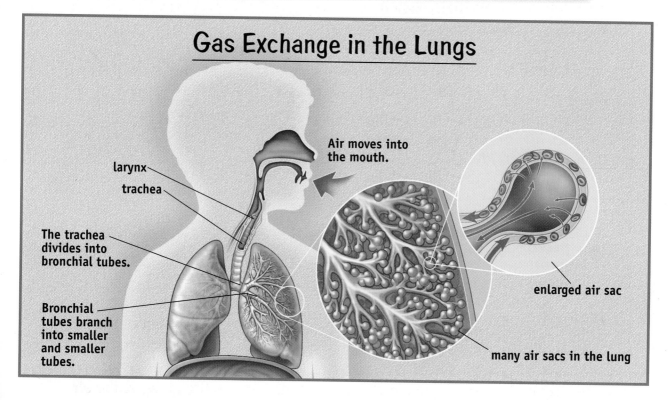

Gas Exchange in the Lungs

larynx

trachea

Air moves into the mouth.

The trachea divides into bronchial tubes.

Bronchial tubes branch into smaller and smaller tubes.

enlarged air sac

many air sacs in the lung

Imagine that you're going to dive into a deep pool. Inhale and hold your breath for as long as you can. At some point, probably within a minute, you have no choice—the muscles in your chest force you to breathe. This is your body's response to the fact that cells could soon be in danger of injury. They need oxygen for energy. And they must get rid of waste gases that are building up. Breathing meets both these needs.

The Bronchial Network

How does the oxygen you inhale get to the cells that need it? After passing through the nose or mouth, air enters the larynx (lar'iŋks), or voice box. The **larynx** is the part of the throat that is used in speaking.

Look at the drawing and find the parts described here. Below the larynx is the trachea. In the middle of the chest, the trachea splits to form two **bronchial tubes**. The bronchial tubes carry air from the trachea to the lungs. One tube enters each lung. Inside the lungs the bronchial tubes branch out into smaller and smaller tubes, much as tree branches do. The branches get smaller until they are like the tiniest twigs. Each twig ends in a tiny air sac.

Through the Wall

The spongy tissue of the lungs has millions of tiny air sacs. These **air sacs** are thin-walled chambers through which oxygen moves into the blood. Around the thin wall of each air sac is a network of tiny blood vessels. Oxygen from inhaled air passes into the air sacs, through the thin walls, and into blood vessels. Here the oxygen is picked up by the blood. Once oxygen passes into the blood, it is carried to the cells where it is needed.

For the air sacs to do their jobs, their walls must be kept clean. For example, when the walls become coated with tobacco smoke, they cannot take in enough oxygen. These delicate air sacs can also be injured by particles in air, called air pollutants, that are breathed in.

An Even Exchange

To release the energy in digested nutrients, cells need oxygen. In releasing this energy, the cells produce a waste product, the gas carbon dioxide. This gas can be dangerous to the cells. In fact, too much of it can poison them. When the blood delivers oxygen to the cells, it takes back the carbon dioxide that is given off. The carbon dioxide is carried by the blood back to the air sacs in the lung.

An exchange of gases takes place in the air sacs. The inhaled air brings oxygen to the air sacs in the lung. As oxygen passes from the air sacs to the blood, carbon dioxide passes from the blood to the air that fills the air sacs.

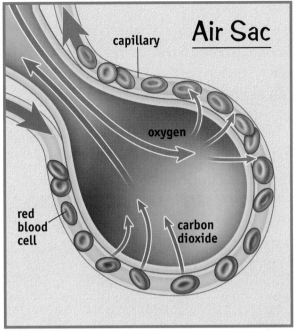

▲ **Gas exchange in an air sac**

Out With the Old

Next, the carbon dioxide in the air sacs must be pushed out of the body. When you hold your breath, the buildup of carbon dioxide signals your body to breathe. From the air sacs, the air passes through the bronchial tubes. After passing through the trachea, it travels through the larynx and out through the mouth or nose.

Exhaled air contains less oxygen than inhaled air and more carbon dioxide than inhaled air. If you breathe on a mirror, you'll notice that the exhaled air also picks up water vapor inside the body. Breathe on a mirror and see for yourself!

Internet Field Trip
Visit **www.eduplace.com** to learn more about the human body.

How You Say It

Moving air allows you to speak. Air flowing through the larynx helps you produce speech sounds. Notice your breathing as you speak. Are you inhaling or exhaling? You need exhaled air to speak.

In the larynx are bands of tissue called vocal cords, shown below. If they are stretched tightly, air flowing between them makes them vibrate. When they vibrate, they produce sounds. Find the larynx in the drawing. Then find your own larynx and place your hand over it. Make a sound. When the sound begins, you'll feel a vibration in the larynx.

When you speak, the muscles in your larynx stretch the vocal cords. Stretched tightly, they are close together. Exhaled air passing through the larynx makes the vocal cords vibrate, producing sound.

Both the respiratory and digestive systems need a way to transport substances to the cells. In the next chapter you'll learn about this transport system.

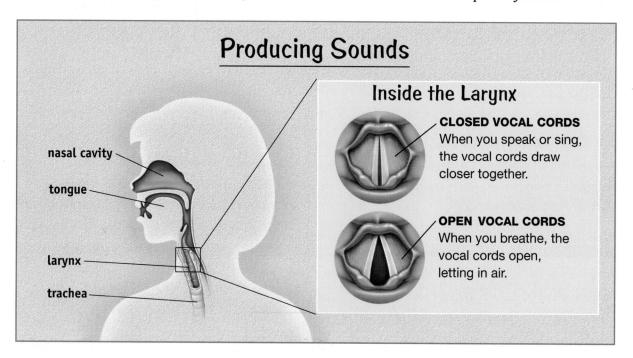

Producing Sounds

nasal cavity

tongue

larynx

trachea

Inside the Larynx

CLOSED VOCAL CORDS
When you speak or sing, the vocal cords draw closer together.

OPEN VOCAL CORDS
When you breathe, the vocal cords open, letting in air.

INVESTIGATION 2 WRAP-UP

THINK IT WRITE IT

REVIEW

1. Starting with the nose, list the main parts of the respiratory system.

2. Describe gas exchange in the air sacs.

CRITICAL THINKING

3. Describe the movement of the lungs and diaphragm when you exhale and when you inhale. Relate this to air flow into and out of the body.

4. During exercise, breathing rate increases. How would you expect an increase in the breathing rate to affect the heart rate? Give reasons for your answer.

REFLECT & EVALUATE

Word Power

Write the letter of the term that best matches the definition. *Not all terms will be used.*

1. The long, coiled organ where most digestion takes place
2. A watery liquid that moistens the mouth and food
3. The air passage connecting the throat to the lungs
4. The muscular tube that connects the mouth to the stomach
5. Looplike structures through which dissolved nutrients pass into the blood

a. bronchial tubes
b. esophagus
c. large intestine
d. peristalsis
e. saliva
f. small intestine
g. trachea
h. villi

Check What You Know

Write the term in each pair that best completes each sentence.

1. When you exhale, you release (oxygen, carbon dioxide).
2. The teeth used mainly for grinding are the (incisors, molars).
3. A tough, but bendable, body material is (mucus, cartilage).
4. When you inhale, the diaphragm moves (up, down).

Problem Solving

1. Imagine that you've just taken a bite out of an apple. Describe what happens to this apple as it moves from your mouth through your digestive system.

2. Pneumonia causes liquids to build up in the air sacs. Based on what you've learned, describe how pneumonia can affect gas exchange. Explain how this might affect the entire body.

BUILD YOUR PORTFOLIO

Copy this drawing of an air sac in the lungs. Explain what the disklike objects are and why they are in different colors. Then explain what the arrows show about gas exchange in the air sac.

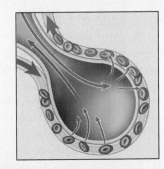

CHAPTER 3

CIRCULATION AND EXCRETION

Your body has a network of connecting tubes that are part of a transport system. These tubes carry materials vital to your body's cells. In this chapter you will explore the transport system's role in supplying needed materials to cells and in removing waste products from those cells.

PEOPLE USING SCIENCE

Medical Illustrator You can see the work of Richard LaRocco on many pages in Chapters 2 and 3 of this unit. He is a medical illustrator, an artist who specializes in drawings of the human body systems. By the age of 16, Richard LaRocco had decided to pursue art as a career. His art teacher, Mrs. Brosch, encouraged him to take art seriously and to develop his skills. His college studies at the Rochester Institute of Technology included human anatomy, medical illustration, and graphic design.

In his work, Richard LaRocco often begins with a paper-and-pencil sketch. Then he goes "high-tech." He scans the art into a computer and completes the work with an "electronic pen." Thinking about art as a career? Richard LaRocco's advice: Learn to draw very well and draw all the time!

Coming Up

◀ Richard LaRocco at work on a drawing of the upper digestive system

HOW DOES THE CIRCULATORY SYSTEM WORK?

The circulatory system, the body's transport system, has three main parts—the heart, the blood vessels, and the blood. In this investigation you'll explore how these three parts work together to transport nutrients and remove wastes.

Activity

Squeeze Play!

How hard does a human heart work to pump blood? Try this activity and find out!

MATERIALS
- rubber ball
- timer
- *Science Notebook*

Procedure

Squeeze a rubber ball hard and then release it. **Predict** how many times you can squeeze the ball in one minute. **Record** your prediction in your *Science Notebook*. While a group member times you, count how many times you can squeeze the ball in one minute. **Record** the number. Repeat this two more times. Next, try to squeeze the ball 70 times in one minute. See how long you can continue at that rate. **Record** your results. **Compare** your results with those of other groups.

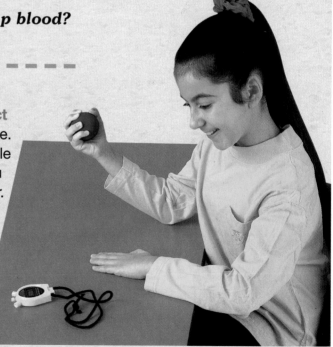

Analyze and Conclude

1. On average, the heart beats about 70 times per minute. How long could you squeeze the ball at the rate of 70 squeezes per minute without stopping?

2. What does this activity tell you about the heart?

Activity

In a Heartbeat

You've learned that the average person's heart beats about 70 times each minute. Find out how hard your own heart is working and what factors affect it.

MATERIALS

- timer
- *Science Notebook*

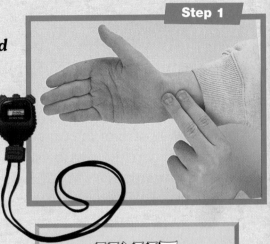

Step 1

Procedure

1. Find your pulse in your wrist, as shown. The **pulse** is the throbbing you can feel in a blood vessel caused by the beating of your heart.

2. Count how many times your heart beats in one minute. This is your heartbeat rate. **Record** this number in your *Science Notebook*.

3. Repeat step 2 two more times. Find the average of the three rates. **Record** the average heartbeat rate.

See **SCIENCE** *and* **MATH TOOLBOX** page H5 if you need to review **Finding an Average.**

4. **Predict** whether your heartbeat rate will change if you exercise. **Record** what you think the rate for one minute will be after exercising.

5. Run in place for one minute. Immediately afterward, find your heartbeat rate as you did in step 2. Then rest for five minutes.

6. Repeat step 5 two more times. Find and **record** the average of the three heartbeat rates.

Analyze and Conclude

1. **Compare** your average heartbeat rate before and after exercising.

2. **Infer** why exercise would cause changes in your heartbeat rate.

UNIT PROJECT LINK

For your chosen plant, research the system that allows for transport of water, minerals, and sugars. Then research the circulatory system in the two animals chosen. Compare these three systems. How are they alike? How are they different? Add materials, such as models or posters, to your display that show how these systems compare.

Technology *Link*

For more help with your Unit Project, go to **www.eduplace.com**.

The Circulatory System

Reading Focus What is the job of the circulatory system?

The **circulatory system** is the transport system of the human body. It carries oxygen and nutrients to all cells and then removes carbon dioxide and other wastes. There are three main parts to this system—the heart, the blood vessels, and the blood. The **heart** is the pump that pushes the blood throughout the entire system. A vast network of tubes, called blood vessels, carries the blood. **Blood** is a tissue made up of a liquid called plasma and several types of cells. Blood carries materials to and from the body's cells.

Look at the drawing below to find the main organs of the circulatory system. Then follow the steps to see how blood circulates throughout the body.

The Circulatory System

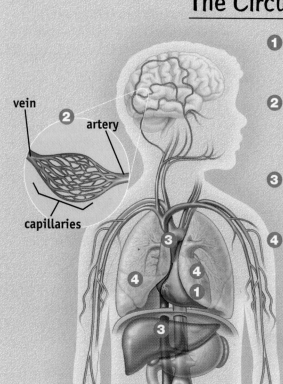

vein

artery

capillaries

1. The left side of the heart pumps oxygen-rich blood through arteries, which carry the blood to all parts of the body.

2. Blood from the arteries enters tiny capillaries. In the capillaries, oxygen and nutrients move to the cells. Wastes, including the waste gas carbon dioxide, move from the cells into the capillaries.

3. Veins carry blood with wastes and carbon dioxide to the right side of the heart. The right side of the heart pumps blood to the lungs.

4. In the lungs, carbon dioxide is exchanged for inhaled oxygen. The oxygen-rich blood moves from the lungs to the heart. From there it is again pumped to the arteries.

▪ ARTERIES carry blood away from heart.

▪ VEINS carry blood to the heart.

▪ CAPILLARIES connect arteries to veins.

A56

Circulation in the Heart

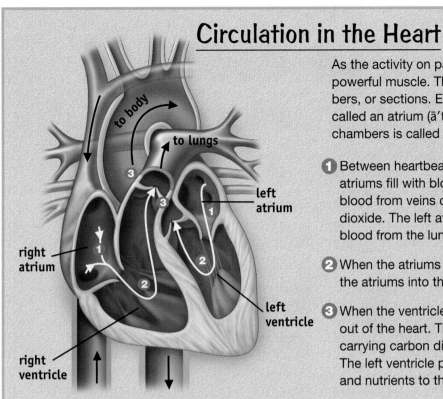

to body

to lungs

left atrium

right atrium

left ventricle

right ventricle

As the activity on page A54 shows, the heart is a powerful muscle. The heart consists of four chambers, or sections. Each of the two top chambers is called an atrium (ā′trē əm). Each of the two lower chambers is called a ventricle (ven′tri kəl).

1 Between heartbeats, the heart relaxes and both atriums fill with blood. The right atrium fills with blood from veins carrying wastes and carbon dioxide. The left atrium fills with oxygen-rich blood from the lungs.

2 When the atriums contract, blood is forced from the atriums into the ventricles.

3 When the ventricles contract, they pump blood out of the heart. The right ventricle pumps blood carrying carbon dioxide and wastes to the lungs. The left ventricle pumps blood carrying oxygen and nutrients to the rest of the body.

The Blood-Vessel Network

The blood vessels form a network through which the heart pumps blood. There are three kinds of blood vessels— arteries, capillaries, and veins.

Arteries are blood vessels that carry blood away from the heart. Most arteries carry oxygen-rich blood, which is bright red. The thick, muscular walls of the arteries stretch when the heart pumps blood into them. Large arteries branch many times into smaller arteries.

The smallest arteries lead into tiny blood vessels called **capillaries**. The capillaries connect the smallest arteries with the smallest veins. Look at the capillaries in the inset drawing on page A56. What happens inside the capillaries?

Veins carry blood from the capillaries to the heart. As blood travels to the heart, the many small veins join to form large veins, much like streams join to form rivers.

Blood and Its Parts

Blood is a fluid made up of blood cells and platelets in a pale yellow liquid called plasma. Plasma contains water, nutrients, wastes, and salts. Red blood cells give blood its color. They carry oxygen from the lungs to the body's cells. They carry carbon dioxide back to the lungs. White blood cells fight germs and break down dead cells. The number of white cells increases when the body is fighting infection. Platelets are tiny discs in plasma that help the blood clot, or thicken.

The Pulse

Your arteries expand and contract as blood pushes through them. You can feel a throbbing where arteries are close to the skin. The throbbing caused by blood rushing into the arteries when the lower chambers of the heart contract is called a **pulse**. Pulse rate is measured in the activity on page A55. ■

Ancient Blood Transfusions

> **Reading Focus** Why could the Incas safely receive blood more than 500 years ago?

Why would a medical treatment work well in one part of the world and have mixed results in another? This medical mystery stumped scientists until they learned more about blood.

Early Transfusions

The mystery begins more than 500 years ago with the Incas. The Incas were a group of people who lived along the western coast of South America. Inca doctors learned how to give blood transfusions to injured people who had lost a lot of blood. A blood transfusion is the transfer of blood from one person to another person. Inca doctors let the blood pass from a blood vessel of a healthy person, through a tube, to a blood vessel of an injured person. This was often a lifesaving measure.

When blood transfusions were tried in Europe in the 1600s, many patients died. In 1818 an English doctor, James Blundell, saved 11 of 15 patients by giving them blood. He noticed that when transfusions failed, the blood cells in the patient were stuck together.

Blood Types

In 1901 the mystery began to unfold. Karl Landsteiner, an Austrian-born doctor working in the United States, found that there are several types of human blood. He named these blood types A, B, AB, and O. He also learned that a **recipient** (ri sip′ē ənt), a person who receives blood, can only safely be given blood of a certain type. Blood from the **donor**, the person who gives blood, must be matched to the recipient's blood. If the blood types don't match, the blood cells clump, or stick together. This clumping of cells causes illness or death.

Look at the table on page A59 to see which recipients can receive blood from which donors. What clues does the table give for solving the mystery?

▲ Machu Picchu, the site of ancient Inca ruins

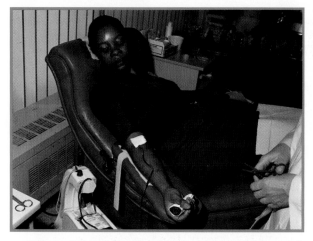
▲ When blood is donated, it is also typed.

▲ Blood cells clumped in mismatched blood

Scientists now think the reason the Incas were successful in blood transfusions was that most of them had type O blood. In western Europe the most common blood types were A and O. It's likely that many early blood transfusions in western Europe failed because of mismatched blood, which caused the blood cells to stick together.

Today, blood is typed when it's drawn. That means it's tested to find out what type it is. Then each unit of blood is labeled by type. As a safety

Blood Types	
Recipient (receives blood)	**Donor** (gives blood)
A	A or O
B	B or O
AB	A, B, AB, or O
O	O

measure, some donor red blood cells are mixed in a tube with some of the patient's plasma. If these mixed cells clump, the blood isn't used. ■

INVESTIGATION 1 WRAP-UP

THINK IT WRITE IT

REVIEW

1. What are the main parts of blood? Briefly describe each part.

2. Name and describe the three types of blood vessels.

CRITICAL THINKING

3. How does the blood entering the right atrium differ from the blood entering the left atrium? Account for the difference.

4. One blood type is called the "universal donor." From the table above, tell which blood type is the universal donor and explain what is meant by that term.

HOW DOES THE EXCRETORY SYSTEM WORK?

Your body gets energy when it "burns" nutrients. Just as burning wood produces ash, "burning" nutrients produces wastes in your body. In this investigation you'll find out about a body system that gets rid of body wastes, such as water and salts.

Activity

MATERIALS
- hand lens
- *Science Notebook*

Peering at Pores

Skin is the largest body part. How does it help you get rid of wastes? Find out.

- -

Procedure

Observe the skin on your arms and hands with a hand lens. In your *Science Notebook,* record all the features you observe. Make a sketch of what you see through the hand lens. Then compare observations with your group members. As a group, list the things the skin does for the body. Record your group's list. Give reasons for each item you put on the list. Compare your list with those of other groups.

Analyze and Conclude

1. What are some of the features you saw on your skin? What do you think these features do for the body?

2. How do you think the skin helps the body get rid of wastes?

Activity

Your Watery Body

Your body needs water to help it get rid of wastes. You take in much of this water in the liquids that you drink. In this activity you'll measure how much liquid you drink in one day.

MATERIALS

- metric measuring cup
- plastic cup
- marker
- *Science Notebook*

Procedure

1. **Predict** how much liquid you'll drink in one day. Include all liquids. **Record** your prediction in your *Science Notebook*.

2. **Make a chart** like the one shown below.

Drinks in a Day		
Time	Type of Liquid	mL of Liquid

3. Make a plastic cup into a liquids measurer. Use a measuring cup to add 50 mL of water to the plastic cup. Use a marker to mark the water line. Label this mark *50 mL*. Add another 50 mL and mark the new water line. Label this mark *100 mL*. Continue marking the cup in this way to its top. Use your liquids measurer as your drinking glass for one day.

 See **SCIENCE** and **MATH TOOLBOX** *page H7 if you need to review **Measuring Volume**.*

4. In your chart, **record** all the liquids you drink during one day. **Record** the time you drink the liquid, the type of liquid, and the amount. Rinse out the measurer each time you use it.

5. **Compare** your results with those of other students.

Analyze and Conclude

1. How much liquid did you drink during the day?

2. Was your intake of liquid about the same as, more than, or less than that of other students?

INVESTIGATE FURTHER!

RESEARCH

Find out how much liquid doctors think a person should drink each day. Research what effect a person's age, weight, health, and activity have on the amount of liquid suggested. Find out the percentage of water in common foods and research the percentage of water in a human body.

The Excretory System

Reading Focus How does the body get rid of wastes?

Your body is constantly busy—even while you are asleep. It is building and replacing cells, releasing energy from food, and maintaining parts that keep the body running smoothly.

All this activity creates body wastes. The human body has a system for ridding itself of harmful wastes produced by the cells. This system is called the **excretory** (eks'krə tôr ē) **system**. The picture below shows the main parts of the excretory system.

Notice that the excretory system includes organs that are part of other body systems. The lungs are part of the respiratory system. But they also

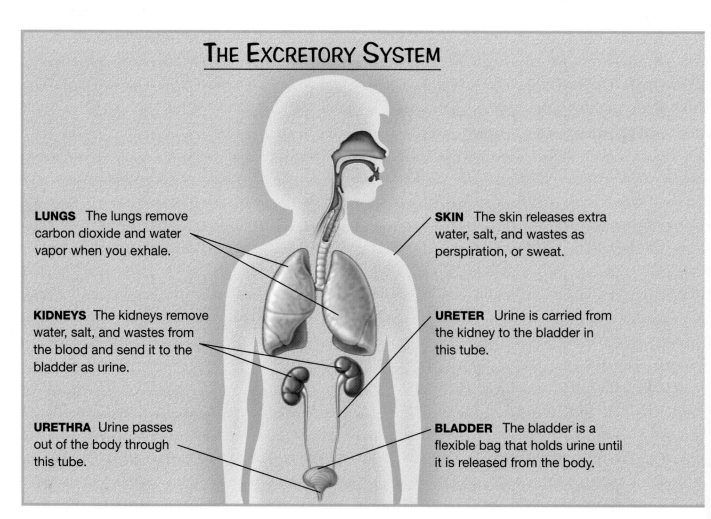

THE EXCRETORY SYSTEM

LUNGS The lungs remove carbon dioxide and water vapor when you exhale.

SKIN The skin releases extra water, salt, and wastes as perspiration, or sweat.

KIDNEYS The kidneys remove water, salt, and wastes from the blood and send it to the bladder as urine.

URETER Urine is carried from the kidney to the bladder in this tube.

URETHRA Urine passes out of the body through this tube.

BLADDER The bladder is a flexible bag that holds urine until it is released from the body.

remove many wastes in exhaled air. For example, the lungs remove excess water. It leaves the body as water vapor, or water in the form of a gas.

But the major waste-removal job of the lungs is to release the wastes formed when carbohydrates and fats are broken down in the cells of the body. Carbohydrates and fats are broken down by oxygen, releasing energy. The carbon in these materials combines with the oxygen to produce carbon dioxide, a waste gas. The carbon dioxide passes into the blood. Then the blood carries this waste gas to the lungs. From the lungs the carbon dioxide is exhaled.

How the Kidneys Work

The **kidneys** are two organs that clean and filter the blood. The filtering of the blood results in the yellowish liquid called **urine** (yŏŏr' in). Kidneys remove excess water and salts. They also remove the wastes that are produced when proteins are broken down into smaller molecules.

From the drawing on page A62 you can see the location of the kidneys. They lie on either side of the spine. Each kidney weighs less than 0.225 kg (about 0.5 lb) and is about the size of a fist.

The drawing on this page shows a closeup of one of millions of tiny filtering units in the kidney. These units, or nephrons (nef'ränz), are found in the outer layer of the kidney. Each unit has a cup-shaped end packed with a tightly coiled ball of capillaries.

Blood passes through the nephron and is filtered under pressure, removing wastes and water. The filtering of blood by the nephron produces urine. The urine drains out of the filtering units into tubes in the middle part of the kidney. From there the urine drains through larger tubes into the bladder, where it collects. Small round muscles keep the urine in the bladder until it is ready to be emptied. When about 250 mL (1 c) of urine has collected, a person has an urge to empty the bladder.

On average, an adult passes about 1.5 L (1.6 qt) of urine per day. Only a small fraction of the water filtered by the kidneys passes into the urine. To help keep a healthy balance of fluids, the kidneys send most of the water and some salt and nutrients back to the blood.

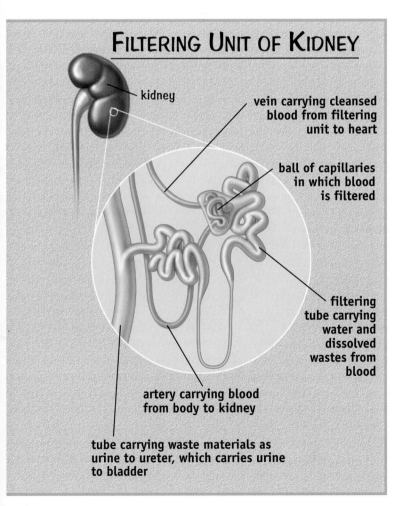

FILTERING UNIT OF KIDNEY

kidney

vein carrying cleansed blood from filtering unit to heart

ball of capillaries in which blood is filtered

filtering tube carrying water and dissolved wastes from blood

artery carrying blood from body to kidney

tube carrying waste materials as urine to ureter, which carries urine to bladder

The Skin

A person also loses water and wastes through the skin. Weighing about 4 kg to 7 kg (9 lb to 15 lb) in an adult, the skin is the largest organ in the body.

The skin removes wastes and water by perspiring, or sweating. Sweating is the release of water, salts, and wastes through pores in the skin. Look at the drawing below. Notice the **sweat glands**, which are small coiled tubes that end at pores on the skin's surface. These pores can be observed in the activity on page A60.

The main function of sweating is to cool the body. When the body produces extra heat, such as during exercise, the circulatory system delivers more blood to the capillaries near the skin. Water, carrying heat, passes into the skin tissues and moves to the sweat glands. This water then reaches the skin surface as perspiration, or sweat. As water evaporates from the skin, it removes some of the heat from the body.

Sometimes a person can lose too much water, salt, and minerals through sweating. Working hard in hot weather, a person can lose as much as 3 L (3 qt) of water! The kidneys can adjust the level of water in the body. But a person needs to drink extra water on a hot day or after exercise to replace the lost water. ■

Internet Field Trip

Visit **www.eduplace.com** to learn more about human body systems.

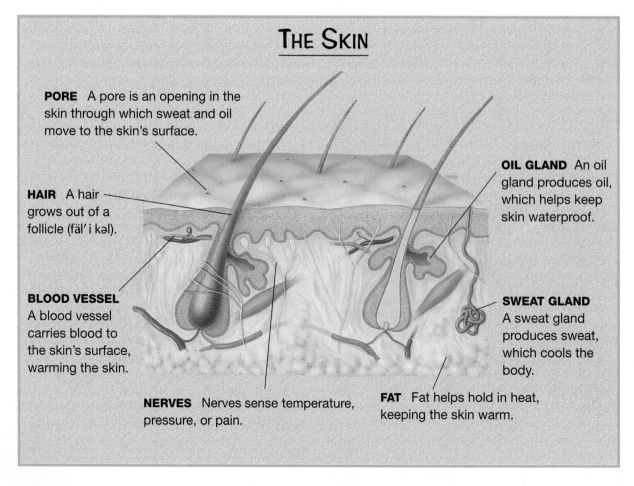

THE SKIN

PORE A pore is an opening in the skin through which sweat and oil move to the skin's surface.

HAIR A hair grows out of a follicle (fäl′ i kəl).

BLOOD VESSEL A blood vessel carries blood to the skin's surface, warming the skin.

OIL GLAND An oil gland produces oil, which helps keep skin waterproof.

SWEAT GLAND A sweat gland produces sweat, which cools the body.

NERVES Nerves sense temperature, pressure, or pain.

FAT Fat helps hold in heat, keeping the skin warm.

Goose Bumps

Reading Focus What causes goose bumps, and how are they helpful?

 Does your skin get covered with little bumps when you are cold or frightened? You probably call these bumps "goose bumps" or "goose pimples." Are goose bumps helpful? Look at the pictures on page A66 to see what causes them. These pictures show two sections of skin. On the left is warm skin. On the right is cold skin.

When you are cold, several things occur. Nerves in the skin signal the brain that it's cold. Small muscles at the bottom of each hair contract, pulling each hair straight up. At the same time, blood vessels near the skin's surface become narrower. Blood flows through blood vessels that are deep within the skin. This process helps to keep the skin warm.

When all the hairs on the skin stand on end, they trap air close to the skin's surface. This layer of trapped air helps to keep the skin warm. As the hair stands straight up, it pulls on the skin

Science in Literature

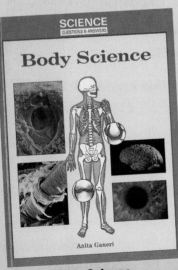

Body Science
by Anita Ganeri
Dillon Press, 1992

WHY IS BLOOD RED?

"Your red blood cells contain a special substance called hemoglobin, which carries oxygen around your body and also gives blood its red color. As your blood flows through your lungs, the hemoglobin takes in oxygen and carries it throughout your body. When the hemoglobin is filled with fresh oxygen, it looks red."

Do you have more questions about your blood and your heart? Many of your questions will be answered by this colorful and informative book. Check out *Body Science* by Anita Ganeri.

around it, forming a bump. This bump is the goose bump!

Do other animals besides humans get goose bumps? Yes! Animals with fur or hair also get cold. When this happens, the hair or fur stands straight up, trapping air that helps to keep the animal warm. Now think about a frightened animal, such as a cat. The fur on a frightened cat fluffs out. This makes the cat look bigger to its enemies. The cat's enemies may stay away if the cat looks scary.

Since humans don't have a thick coat of fur or hair, goose bumps don't do a lot to keep them warm. But goose bumps can let you know when it's time to put on a sweater or to stop watching a scary movie! ■

 Using Math *What Celsius temperatures might cause the reactions shown? What Fahrenheit temperatures might do the same?*

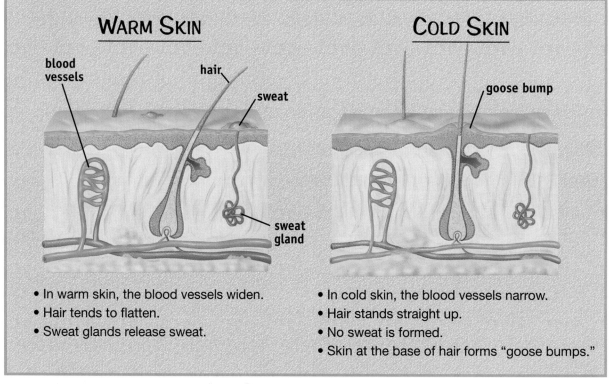

WARM SKIN

blood vessels
hair
sweat
sweat gland

- In warm skin, the blood vessels widen.
- Hair tends to flatten.
- Sweat glands release sweat.

COLD SKIN

goose bump

- In cold skin, the blood vessels narrow.
- Hair stands straight up.
- No sweat is formed.
- Skin at the base of hair forms "goose bumps."

INVESTIGATION 2 WRAP-UP

 **THINK IT WRITE IT**

REVIEW

1. List and describe the three main parts of the excretory system. Explain the function of each part.

2. Describe what happens in a filtering unit of the kidney.

CRITICAL THINKING

3. Explain why the skin can be thought of as part of the excretory system.

4. How is a bird with fluffed-up feathers like a person with goose bumps?

REFLECT & EVALUATE

Word Power

Write the letter of the term that best matches the definition. *Not all terms will be used.*

1. A tissue that carries materials to and from the body's cells
2. Blood vessels that carry blood from the capillaries to the heart
3. Blood vessels that carry blood away from the heart
4. A pair of organs that clean and filter the blood
5. A person who gives blood for transfusions
6. Blood vessels that connect the smallest arteries with the smallest veins

a. arteries
b. blood
c. capillaries
d. donor
e. heart
f. kidneys
g. recipient
h. veins

Check What You Know

Write the term in each pair that best completes each statement.

1. Urine passes out of the body through the (ureter, urethra).
2. Tiny discs that help blood to clot are called (platelets, pores).
3. The two lower chambers of the heart are the (atriums, ventricles).

Problem Solving

1. Explain how the filtering units of the kidneys are somewhat like the air sacs in the lungs.

2. While fixing his bicycle, a boy cut a large blood vessel in his hand. Every few seconds, the blood would spurt out. What would this tell you about the kind of blood vessel that was cut? Explain your answer.

BUILD YOUR PORTFOLIO

Copy this drawing of the excretory system. Identify parts *a–e*. Briefly describe the function of each part. Which of these parts also belongs to another body system? Name that system.

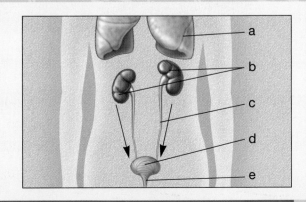

CHAPTER 4

LIFE CYCLES

All living things pass through a life cycle. They might crack out of an eggshell or sprout from a seed. Some live only a few days; others live more than one hundred years. In this chapter you'll explore the life cycle of several different animals and plants.

PEOPLE USING SCIENCE

Animal Nutritionist Dr. Diane A. Hirakawa is a specialist in the field of animal nutrition. She develops tasty, nutritious pet food suited to the age, activity, and health of pets. "Animals always greet you with a wag of a tail or a lick on the face," writes Dr. Hirakawa, who chose her career because she loves animals.

Dr. Hirakawa is Senior Vice President of Research and Development at The Iams Company, producers of pet foods. To prepare for her career, Dr. Hirakawa studied companion animal biology in college. Then she earned a Ph.D. in nutritional biochemistry. In 1995 she coauthored a book on animal nutrition. Her book deals with dietary needs of animals at different stages in their life cycle.

▲ These dogs are eating food suited to the life cycle stage they are in.

WHAT ARE THE STAGES IN AN ANIMAL'S LIFE CYCLE?

Are there any babies in your family? Are there any people older than 80? All living things pass through stages. In this investigation you'll explore the life cycle of several different animals.

Activity

Life Cycle of a Brine Shrimp

Do animals change as they age? What is the importance of change in the life of an animal? By observing changes in the life of a tiny animal, the brine shrimp, you'll discover answers to some of these questions.

Procedure

1. Obtain some brine shrimp eggs from your teacher. Use a hand lens and microscope to examine the eggs. Note their size, color, and texture. **Record** your observations in your *Science Notebook*.

See **SCIENCE** *and* **MATH TOOLBOX** page H2 if you need to review *Using a Microscope.*

2. With your group, **brainstorm** questions about how the brine shrimp grow and develop. **Record** your questions.

MATERIALS

- brine shrimp eggs
- hand lens
- microscope
- plastic cup
- salt water
- measuring cup
- red marker
- dried powdered yeast
- dropper
- plastic teaspoon
- microscope slides
- cover slip
- *Science Notebook*

SAFETY

Wash your hands before and after working with brine shrimp. Clean up spills immediately.

3. Prepare an egg hatchery. Obtain room-temperature salt water from your teacher. Add 250 mL of this water to a plastic cup. With a red marker, mark the level of water on the outside of the cup.

4. Sprinkle one fourth of a teaspoon of brine shrimp eggs into the cup. Check with your teacher. You may need to add a pinch of yeast to the water as food for the brine shrimp. Stir the mixture. Place the hatchery in a warm place, where it will not be disturbed.

5. Make a chart like the one shown below. Leave enough space to record three weeks of observations.

Step 7

Date	Observations	Drawing

6. Observe the egg hatchery the next day. Record your observations.

7. Each day for three weeks, use a dropper to carefully remove a few eggs. Observe them with a hand lens and through a microscope. Record any changes you notice. Draw what you see when you observe the brine shrimp with the hand lens and the microscope. Return the brine shrimp you observe to the plastic cup. As water evaporates from the cup, add salt water up to the red line.

8. Compare your observations with those of other members of your class.

Analyze and Conclude

1. What stages of development did you observe in the brine shrimp?

2. Were your questions about the brine shrimp's growth answered by the activity? Explain.

3. What changes occurred in the brine shrimp at each stage?

4. What stage was reached by about the twentieth day? Infer why this stage is important.

INVESTIGATE FURTHER!

EXPERIMENT

Can you speed up the life cycle of a brine shrimp? Plan and carry out an experiment that would decrease the number of days needed for eggs to hatch and grow into adults. You may wish to use a computer, including CD-ROM programs, to plan your experiment and to record and analyze your results.

The Human Life Cycle

Reading Focus What are the main stages in the human life cycle?

Where are you in your life cycle? You've changed a lot since you were a tiny baby. Now you're just a couple of years from being a teenager. Find out about the stages that humans pass through from infancy to old age.

Infancy

Infancy is a stage that lasts from birth to about age 1. At birth an infant is almost completely dependent on its parents for survival. Through the first year, the baby gains control of its muscles and other systems. As a baby develops, it can sit up, creep, then crawl, stand, and walk. During this period the infant is growing at a tremendous rate.

An infant shows traits that are inherited, or passed down, from its parents. For example, the infant might have inherited straight black hair from its father and dimples from its mother.

Childhood

Childhood is a stage that lasts from about age 1 to about age 12. This stage begins with the ability to walk. Most children learn to walk from 9 months to about 15 months. Through the first year of childhood, the growth spurt of infancy continues. The growth rate is fairly steady from age 4 until age 11 or 12.

▲ The human life cycle

During childhood a person learns many skills that will be used for the rest of life. A child learns how to speak his or her parents' language by imitating what the parents say. A lot is learned from the child's environment. A child may learn about the pain of touching a hot stove. Through such a painful experience, the child learns to stay away from a hot stove.

Adolescence

Adolescence lasts from about age 11 to about age 18 to 20. It is during this stage that a person grows into adulthood. A second growth spurt occurs, and the adult body takes shape. During this stage a person becomes able to reproduce.

Adulthood

Adulthood is the stage that begins at the end of the teenage years and lasts the rest of a person's life. Early in this stage, the body is at the peak of its physical abilities. This is usually when the person has the greatest strength and greatest physical endurance. Responsibilities during this stage may include raising a family and earning a living. Physical ability declines in later adulthood.

In the United States, a male born in 1993 can expect to live an average of 72.2 years. A female born in 1993 can expect to live an average of 78.8 years. As medical science advances, people are able to live longer and more healthfully. ■

The Life Cycle of an Insect

Reading Focus What are the stages in the life cycle of a beetle?

You've learned about the stages in the life cycle of a human. You know that a baby looks somewhat like an adult human being—just much smaller! With some kinds of animals, each stage in the life cycle is very different. The animal looks very different at each stage. It also lives in different places and eats different kinds of food. The beetle, which is an insect, is such an animal.

How a Beetle Changes

A beetle goes through four distinct stages in its life cycle. Animals that go through these four stages are said to pass through **complete metamorphosis** (kəm plēt' met ə môr'fə sis). Refer to the table on page A75 to see what happens at each stage.

The **egg** is the first stage in the beetle's life cycle. An adult beetle lays her eggs in the openings of wet decaying wood or in soil. The **larva**, also called a grub, is the wormlike stage that follows the egg stage. A beetle larva eats wet decaying wood or other rotting material in soil. As the grub eats and develops, it gets larger. Once it reaches a certain size, it molts, or sheds its outer skin. After it molts, the larva comes out, a bit larger than before.

The **pupa** (pyoo'pə) is the stage between the larva and the adult. During this stage, the beetle might look like it's at rest. Actually the insect is going through many changes. It changes color and develops a hard outer case. Adult organs form, and the beetle develops wings. The insect may stay in this stage for a few days or several weeks, depending on the kind of beetle it is. The photograph on this page shows the inside of the pupa case.

The **adult** is the final stage in the beetle's life cycle. The adult beetle comes out of the pupa fully grown. It now has six legs, two pairs of wings, complex mouth parts, and adult organs.

▲ Lengthwise section of a beetle pupa, showing the developing insect

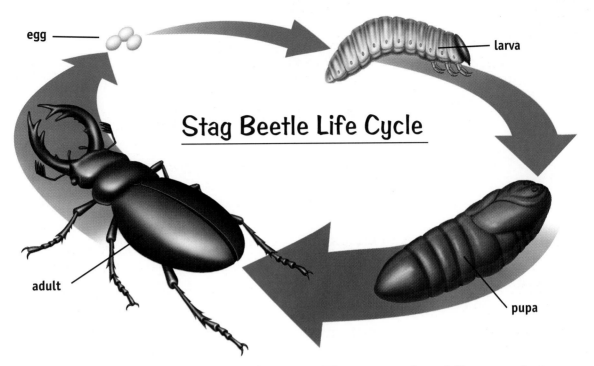

Stag Beetle Life Cycle

egg

larva

pupa

adult

The adult male and adult female beetle mate. Then the female lays her eggs in wet decaying wood. The entire cycle begins again.

The Moth and the Butterfly

Like beetles, moths and butterflies go through complete metamorphosis. They pass through the same four stages—egg, larva, pupa, and adult.

There are a few differences between the life cycles of beetles, moths, and butterflies. The table below shows you these differences and the names given to each of the stages. You are probably most familiar with the terms *cocoon* and *caterpillar*. Notice that the pupa stage of a moth is called a cocoon. The pupa stage of a butterfly is called a chrysalis (kris′ə lis). ■

Life Cycles of Three Insects

Beetle	Moth	Butterfly
egg	egg	egg
larva (grub)	larva (caterpillar)	larva (caterpillar)
pupa	pupa (cocoon)	pupa (chrysalis)
adult (beetle)	adult (moth)	adult (butterfly)

Vertebrate Life Cycles

Reading Focus What are the stages in the life cycles of some vertebrates?

Fish and humans share an important characteristic. A fish, like a human, is a **vertebrate** (vʉr′tə brit), an animal with a backbone. Vertebrates have a series of bones that make up their backbone.

A Fishy Story

Some kinds of fish live in fresh water and some live in salt water. Some kinds live in both fresh water and salt water at different times in their life cycle. The drawings on page A77 show the life cycle of a fish that you might eat for dinner—the salmon.

Adult salmon live in the ocean. When it's time to reproduce, these fish return to the same freshwater stream where they hatched. Salmon may swim as far as 3,220 km (2,000 mi) to where they hatched.

This behavior—returning to the freshwater stream—is instinctive (in stiŋk′tiv)

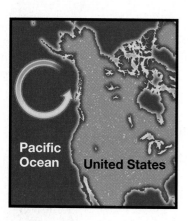

Pacific Ocean United States

◀ The yellow arrow on this map shows the great distance the salmon swims from its hatching place to the ocean and back again.

behavior. It is behavior that the salmon inherits, or is born with. A salmon does not have to learn to do this.

As she prepares to lay her eggs, the adult female salmon forms several nests in the gravel at the bottom of the stream. She lays 2,000 to 17,000 sticky eggs. The adult male salmon releases male sex cells over the eggs.

When a male sex cell joins with an egg, or female sex cell, the result is called a fertilized egg. A young salmon develops from a fertilized egg. Each fertilized egg forms a yolk sac, which is food for the tiny fish.

At the next stage, the salmon looks like a tiny spotted fish. By the time a young salmon is two years old, it takes on the silvery color of the adult fish. It begins the long journey from its freshwater home to the ocean.

After swimming great distances to the ocean, the adult male and female salmon remain in the ocean until they are ready to reproduce. When the females are ready to lay eggs, all adults swim upstream, against the flow of water, to the same freshwater river where they hatched. After the female lays her eggs and the male releases male sex cells over the eggs, the adult salmon die. Then the cycle continues.

A76

Salmon Life Cycle

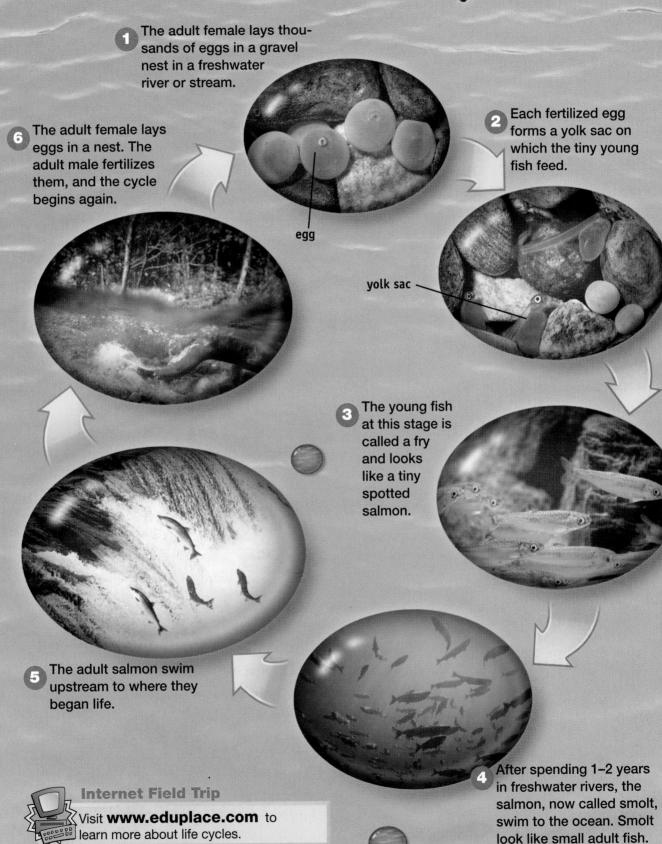

1 The adult female lays thousands of eggs in a gravel nest in a freshwater river or stream.

2 Each fertilized egg forms a yolk sac on which the tiny young fish feed.

6 The adult female lays eggs in a nest. The adult male fertilizes them, and the cycle begins again.

egg

yolk sac

3 The young fish at this stage is called a fry and looks like a tiny spotted salmon.

5 The adult salmon swim upstream to where they began life.

4 After spending 1–2 years in freshwater rivers, the salmon, now called smolt, swim to the ocean. Smolt look like small adult fish.

Internet Field Trip
Visit **www.eduplace.com** to learn more about life cycles.

It's for the Birds

Woodpeckers use their pointed beaks to hunt for insects in bark. They sleep in larger holes that they drill in the sides of trees. Hunting for insects and drilling holes is instinctive. That is, a woodpecker is born with the ability to drill holes. This bird inherits from its parents the ability to drill holes in wood.

Woodpeckers mate for life. After a courtship dance in the spring, a pair of birds mate. Then the female lays up to fourteen eggs in a hole drilled in a tree. Male and female birds take turns sitting on the eggs to warm them. Inside each egg, a tiny woodpecker is developing.

In about 12 days, the young bird pecks open the shell. It comes out with wrinkly pink skin and no feathers. Its eyes don't open for 8 days. The young birds remain in the hole in the tree, and the parent birds bring caterpillars for their young to eat. The parents defend the young birds from enemies. This behavior by the adults is also instinctive. In a couple of weeks, the baby birds have grown feathers. By four weeks of age they are ready to learn to fly and hunt for themselves.

The family remains together throughout the summer. By November the birds are ready to live on their own. Each young woodpecker drills a hole in a tree for shelter and seeks a mate. Next spring the young woodpeckers will reproduce, and the cycle will continue.

Science in Literature

Why Save the Rain Forest?
by Donald Silver
Illustrated by Patricia J. Wynne
Julian Messner, 1993

SECRETS OF SURVIVAL

"When it is time for the butterflies to lay their yellow eggs, the passionflower leaves provide the perfect spot. Once the eggs hatch, the emerging caterpillars chomp into the vine's leaves without being harmed by the poison. Why? The caterpillars are able to store the poison inside their bodies. They use it as a weapon against birds that eat caterpillars. . . ."

Find out about the amazing ways that butterflies survive in the rain forest. Read these stories of survival in *Why Save the Rain Forest?* by Donald Silver.

These eggs will hatch in about twelve days.

Newly hatched birds are blind and helpless.

Very young birds are fed by their parents.

Woodpecker
Life Cycle

An adult woodpecker drills a hole for a nest.

These birds search for insects in a tree trunk.

INVESTIGATION 1 WRAP-UP

THINK IT WRITE IT

REVIEW

1. Describe the four main stages in the life cycle of an insect that goes through complete metamorphosis.

2. Name and describe four stages in the human life cycle. Name a learned and an inherited trait.

CRITICAL THINKING

3. Compare the human life cycle with the bird life cycle. Consider such things as how an infant and a young bird obtain food.

4. Compare the life cycle of a butterfly with that of a beetle. How are they alike? How are they different?

INVESTIGATION 2

WHAT ARE THE STAGES IN A PLANT'S LIFE CYCLE?

Which came first—the acorn or the oak tree? The answer may always be a matter of opinion. In this investigation you'll explore how plants change during their life cycle.

Activity

The Secret of a Seed

You put a seed in soil and keep it moist. In a few days a tiny new plant with roots, a stem, and leaves appears. How can a new living plant come from a seed that seems lifeless? Find out what secrets a seed holds!

Step 3

MATERIALS

- soaked lima bean seeds
- soaked corn kernels
- plastic knife
- hand lens
- toothpicks
- *Science Notebook*

SAFETY

Use care in handling the knife.

Procedure

1. Examine and compare a lima bean seed and a corn kernel, which is actually a corn seed. Record your observations in your *Science Notebook*. Make drawings of the seeds.

2. Carefully peel off the thin outer coverings of a lima bean and a corn kernel. Observe each covering with a hand lens. Record the differences and similarities you see.

3. Gently split open the bean seed with either your fingernail or a plastic knife. Spread open the two halves of the bean seed and **examine** each half with a hand lens. **Draw** what you observe. **Record** your osbservations.

 Math Hint *As you examine each half of the seed, note any symmetric shapes or structures.*

4. **Predict** what you will find inside the corn kernel. Then use the knife to carefully cut the corn kernel in half lengthwise through the side. Lay the halves flat.

5. **Examine** each half with the hand lens. **Compare** the inside of the corn kernel with the inside of the bean seed. **Draw** the inside of the corn kernel. **Discuss** what you have observed with other members of your group.

6. Use a toothpick to scrape off a bit of the material that fills up each seed. **Examine** the material with the hand lens. **Compare** the material from the bean seed with that from the corn seed.

Analyze and Conclude

1. How was the covering of the lima bean seed different from the covering of the corn kernel? How was it similar? **Infer** the purpose that each covering serves.

2. What structures did you find inside each seed?

3. **Hypothesize** the function of the material that fills up each seed.

4. What can you **infer** about seeds from this activity?

UNIT PROJECT LINK

Research the life cycles of the same three organisms you have been using in your museum display. Use posters or models to show how their life cycles compare. Point out how their life cycles are alike and how they are different. Add these materials to your display. Invite other classes to view the completed display.

Technology Link

For more help with your Unit Project, go to **www.eduplace.com**.

Activity

It's Just a Stage

Infant, child, adolescent, adult are the stages of the human life cycle. In this activity you'll use fast-growing radish seeds to find out if plants have similar life-cycle stages.

Procedure

1. Fill a small flowerpot with soil. Place 4 fast-growing radish seeds in the pot, spaced evenly apart near the rim. Cover them lightly with soil. Water the seeds. Using a dropper, add liquid houseplant fertilizer to the soil according to the package directions.

2. Place the flowerpot under a good source of artificial light. Keep the light on 24 hours a day. Check the soil each day, making sure to keep it moist, not wet, at all times. When the seeds sprout, assign each tiny plant a different number to help you keep track of its growth. Write the number on the pot, near each plant.

3. In your *Science Notebook*, make a chart for recording height as the plants grow. Measure and record each plant's height each day. Then make a line graph that shows the growth of each plant. As the plants grow, record your observations and draw the plants.

Plant #	Height (cm)				
	Day 1	Day 2	Day 3	Day 4	Day 5
1					

See **SCIENCE** and **MATH TOOLBOX** page H13 if you need to review *Making a Line Graph.*

Step 4

4. When the stems are 5 cm tall, use a red marker to make a dot on the stem just below the leaves. Each day measure and record the distance between the soil and the dot.

Measure and record the distance at the same time each day.

5. If your plants form flowers, follow your teacher's instructions for using cotton swabs to transfer pollen from the flower of one plant to the flower of another plant. Record your method of pollination.

6. Continue to observe your plants. If fruits are produced, open several when they are ripe and examine the contents.

Analyze and Conclude

1. Seedlings are the tiny plants that first appear above the soil. How many days after planting seeds did most seedlings appear? If you saw flower buds, how many days after planting did they appear? If your plants formed fruits, how many days did it take for them to form fruits with seeds?

2. What can you infer about stem growth from the measurements you made each day?

3. What stages in the life cycle of a plant did you observe?

4. What stage in the plant's life cycle is similar to the life-cycle stage you are in? Explain your answer.

From Flower to Fruit

Reading Focus How do fruits and seeds form from a flower?

How would you encourage someone to visit you? You might prepare some food, put on your best clothes, and make sure you smell good. That's just what many flowers do to attract insects. When an insect visits a flower, however, the visit begins the process that ends with seed production.

The flower is the reproductive organ of a flowering plant. Some kinds of plants have flowers that produce both male and female sex cells. Other kinds have flowers that produce either male or female sex cells. When an insect visits a flower, it transfers the male sex cells from one flower to another. This transfer is part of the process of sexual reproduction in the flower. During **sexual reproduction** a male sex cell joins with a female sex cell to produce a fertilized (fŭrt″l īzd) egg. In flowering plants, this fertilized egg develops into a tiny plant enclosed in a seed. Through sexual reproduction, the tiny plant inherits traits, such as petal color and leaf shape, from each parent plant.

How a Fruit Forms

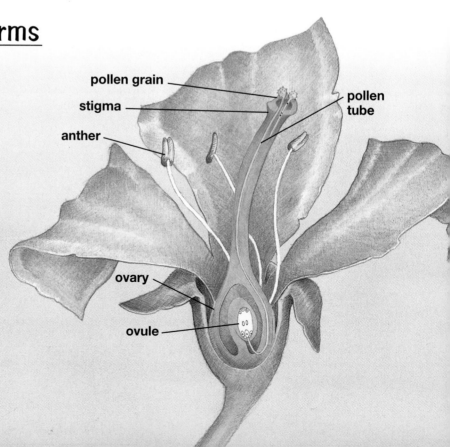

pollen grain

stigma

anther

pollen tube

ovary

ovule

STAMEN The **stamen** is the male part of the flower. It produces pollen.

Anther The anther holds pollen grains, which contain male sex cells.

PISTIL The **pistil** is the female part of a flower.

Stigma The stigma is the sticky part on the top of the pistil to which pollen grains stick.

Ovary The ovary becomes the fruit.

Ovule The ovule produces the female sex cells. If fertilized, the ovule develops into a seed.

Producing Seeds and Fruits

Look at the pictures on pages A84 and A85 to see how seeds and fruits are formed. The first step in producing seeds is the transfer of pollen grains from the male part of a flower (the stamen) to the female part of another flower (the pistil). The **pollen grain** contains the male sex cell. When an insect, a bird, or a bat brushes against an anther, which contains the pollen grains, some of the pollen sticks to the animal's body. As the animal moves to the next flower, some pollen brushes off its body onto the stigma, which is at the tip of the pistil. This transfer of pollen grains is called **pollination** (päl ə nā′shən).

Some flowers are pollinated when wind or rain carries pollen to them from another flower. These flowers usually are not scented or brightly colored. They do not attract animals for pollination.

Pollination can take place only between plants of the same kind. For example, if pollen from an apple blossom lands on a tulip, no pollination occurs. A tulip must be pollinated by pollen grains from another tulip.

Inside the ovule, the fertilized egg forms an **embryo** (em′brē ō), a tiny new plant. Other cells in the ovule produce a food supply for the embryo. The ovule then forms a protective seed coat around the embryo and its food supply, forming a seed. In the activity on pages A80–A81, bean seeds and corn seeds are opened to reveal a tiny embryo and its food supply. Every seed contains these basic parts. The activity on pages A82 and A83 shows the germination of a seed and its growth into a flowering plant. As growth continues, the flower forms a fruit and seeds.

The ovary surrounding the seed or seeds enlarges and develops into a **fruit**. The fruit protects the seeds as they grow. Some fruits, such as cherries, have only one seed; others, such as oranges, have many seeds. ■

1 Pollen grain lands on the stigma of the pistil.

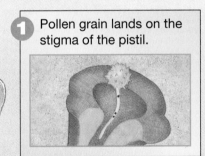

2 A pollen tube grows down into the ovary. **Fertilization** (fʉrt ′l i zā′shən) takes place when a male sex cell from the pollen grain joins with the female sex cell inside the ovary.

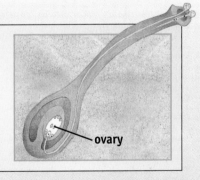

ovary

3 Following fertilization, the ovary enlarges and begins to form a fruit.

ovary

4 The ovary continues to enlarge, and seeds begin to form.

seeds

5 The fruit has ripened and has split open, releasing the seeds.

The Story of a Flowering Tree

Reading Focus What are the main stages in the life cycle of a flowering tree?

The Story of a Flowering Tree

In late spring, red maple seeds ripen and fall off the tree. The seeds are inside the fruit, connected in pairs. A thin "wing" allows the wind to carry the seeds away from the parent tree.

As they fall to the ground, many seeds are eaten or hidden, to be eaten at a later time by insects and small animals, such as squirrels. Some fruits lie on the ground long enough to open and release the seeds.

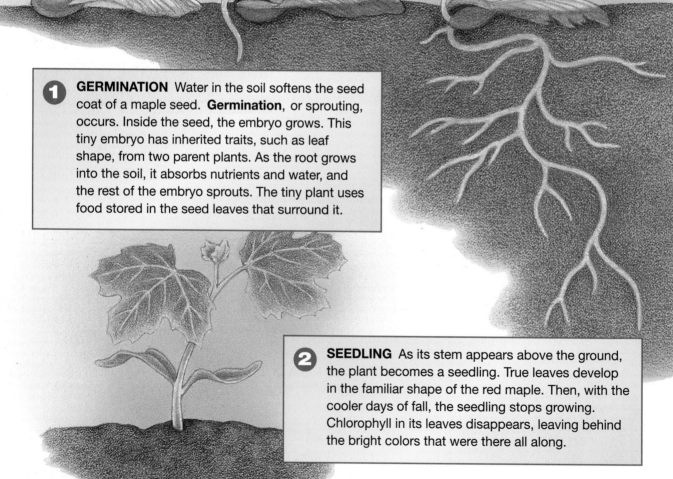

1 **GERMINATION** Water in the soil softens the seed coat of a maple seed. **Germination**, or sprouting, occurs. Inside the seed, the embryo grows. This tiny embryo has inherited traits, such as leaf shape, from two parent plants. As the root grows into the soil, it absorbs nutrients and water, and the rest of the embryo sprouts. The tiny plant uses food stored in the seed leaves that surround it.

2 **SEEDLING** As its stem appears above the ground, the plant becomes a seedling. True leaves develop in the familiar shape of the red maple. Then, with the cooler days of fall, the seedling stops growing. Chlorophyll in its leaves disappears, leaving behind the bright colors that were there all along.

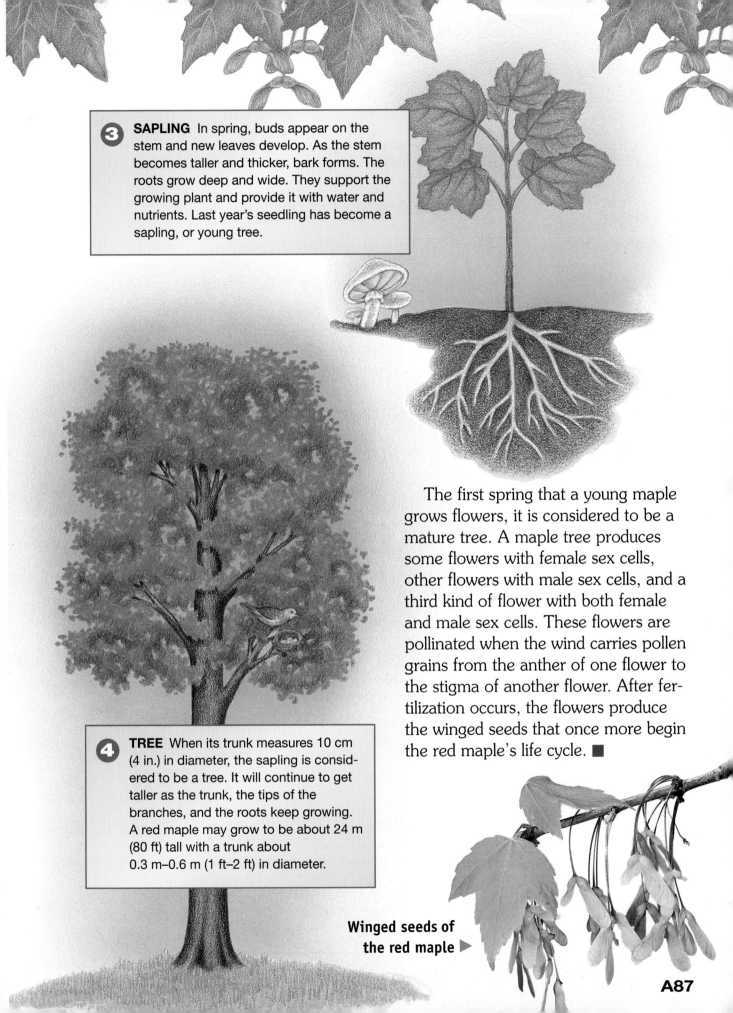

③ SAPLING In spring, buds appear on the stem and new leaves develop. As the stem becomes taller and thicker, bark forms. The roots grow deep and wide. They support the growing plant and provide it with water and nutrients. Last year's seedling has become a sapling, or young tree.

④ TREE When its trunk measures 10 cm (4 in.) in diameter, the sapling is considered to be a tree. It will continue to get taller as the trunk, the tips of the branches, and the roots keep growing. A red maple may grow to be about 24 m (80 ft) tall with a trunk about 0.3 m–0.6 m (1 ft–2 ft) in diameter.

The first spring that a young maple grows flowers, it is considered to be a mature tree. A maple tree produces some flowers with female sex cells, other flowers with male sex cells, and a third kind of flower with both female and male sex cells. These flowers are pollinated when the wind carries pollen grains from the anther of one flower to the stigma of another flower. After fertilization occurs, the flowers produce the winged seeds that once more begin the red maple's life cycle. ■

Winged seeds of the red maple ▶

The Life of a Bristlecone Pine

Reading Focus How long has this bristlecone pine been growing?

One of the oldest living things on Earth is a bristlecone pine named Methuselah. Methuselah has been growing in Great Basin National Park in California's White Mountains for about 4,600 years!

Today only a small portion of Methuselah is still alive. We know how old Methuselah is because scientists used a tiny hollow drill to bore into the tree. They removed a thin core of wood. From this core, they counted the annual rings, which tell the tree's age.

If the twisted, wind-battered tree called Methuselah could talk, what might it tell us about the important events that have occurred during its lifetime? The time line shows some of the events during Methuselah's long life.

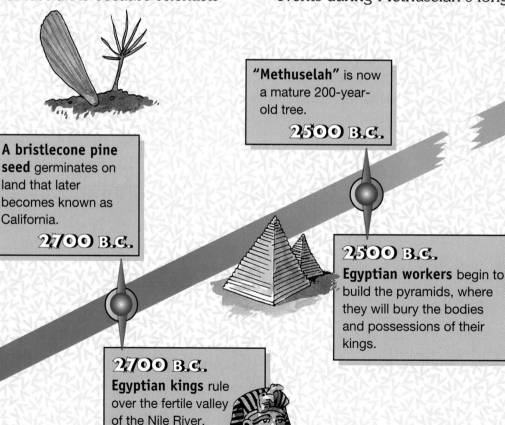

"Methuselah" is now a mature 200-year-old tree.

2500 B.C.

A bristlecone pine seed germinates on land that later becomes known as California.

2700 B.C.

2500 B.C.
Egyptian workers begin to build the pyramids, where they will bury the bodies and possessions of their kings.

2700 B.C.
Egyptian kings rule over the fertile valley of the Nile River.

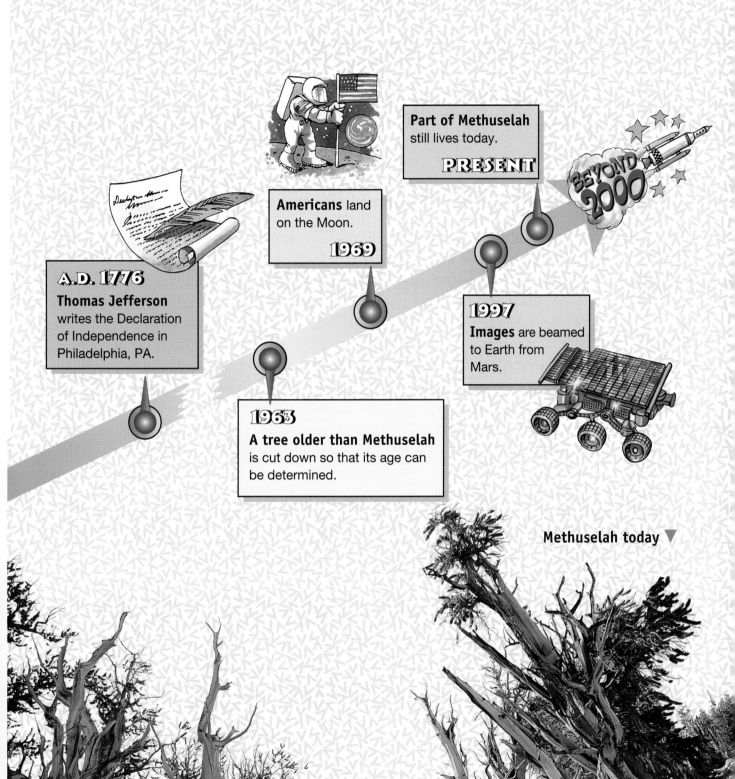

A.D. 1776
Thomas Jefferson writes the Declaration of Independence in Philadelphia, PA.

Americans land on the Moon.
1969

Part of Methuselah still lives today.
PRESENT

BEYOND 2000

1963
A tree older than Methuselah is cut down so that its age can be determined.

1997
Images are beamed to Earth from Mars.

Methuselah today ▼

Growing Plants Without Seeds

Reading Focus What are two ways that new plants can grow without seeds?

SCIENCE TECHNOLOGY & SOCIETY

When you plant seeds, you are planting the result of sexual reproduction—the joining of male and female sex cells from the parent plants. However, you can also grow new plants without using seeds. Such plants are produced by asexual reproduction. In asexual reproduction, offspring are produced from one or more cells of a single parent.

Cuttings

One way to produce new plants without planting seeds is by using cuttings. For example, with some kinds of plants you can cut a length of stem that has one or more leaves. The stem will grow roots when placed in water for a few days or weeks. The rooted stem can then be planted in soil and will grow into an entire new plant. This is a type of asexual reproduction. The new plants grown this way are clones, or exact copies of the parent plants.

Tissue Culture

Another type of asexual reproduction is tissue culture. A group of cells that works together is called a *tissue.* *Culture* is another word for "growing." Tissue culture is growing new plants in the laboratory from the cells of other plants. The growth is done in test tubes or in culture plates.

When might a plant be grown through tissue culture instead of from a seed? Suppose most plants in a crop are affected by a disease. Then one of the plants is found to have a trait making it resistant to disease. Tissue from this healthy plant is grown by means of tissue culture. Since the new plant tissue is exactly like that of the parent plant, the new plants grown are also resistant to disease. Tissue culture can lead to a disease-resistant crop.

A leaf cutting (*left*) and plants grown from tissue culture in test tubes (*right*). ▼

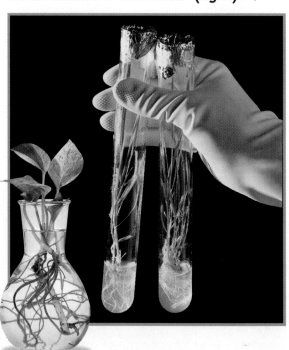

Life Cycle of a Cone Plant

Reading Focus What are the stages in the life cycle of a cone plant?

You've probably seen pine cones lying on the ground beneath a tall pine tree. Have you ever wondered what pine cones are?

Trees that produce cones are called **conifers**. The word *conifer* means "cone-bearing." Conifers have a life cycle that is similar to that of flowering plants. But instead of producing flowers and fruits, they produce cones. Seeds form inside the cones.

A pine is a type of conifer, or cone-producing tree. Both male and female cones grow on a pine tree. Compare the male and female cones in the photograph on this page.

What's in a Cone?

During winter the male cone produces pollen grains. Recall that the pollen grains contain the male sex cells. As the male cones grow in the spring, they open, releasing the pollen grains. Wind carries the pollen grains to the female cone.

In the spring, female cones are soft and green. Like flowers, the female cones contain ovules from which the seeds grow. The female cone produces a sticky material that traps the pollen grains. The process by which pollen grains from the male cone are transferred to the female cone is pollination.

After the pollen becomes trapped in the female cone, a pollen tube grows from the pollen into the ovule. Male sex cells from the pollen travel to the egg inside the ovule. Fertilization occurs when the male sex cell and the female sex cell, or egg, unite. From these two parts, the seed will grow. After fertilization, the female cone grows

Female cone of white pine (*left*); male cones (*right*)

seed ▶

▲ pollen grains

larger, becomes woody, and the spaces between the scales close.

What's in a Seed?

Like a seed in a flowering plant, the seed in a cone plant contains three main parts. It contains an embryo, a layer of food used by the very young plant, and a seed coat that protects the seed.

In the fall the female cone opens and the seeds are released and carried by the wind. Many will be eaten by animals. Those that remain will not germinate until spring. A young tree grows for several years before it is mature and produces cones. When it produces male and female cones, the life cycle begins again. ■

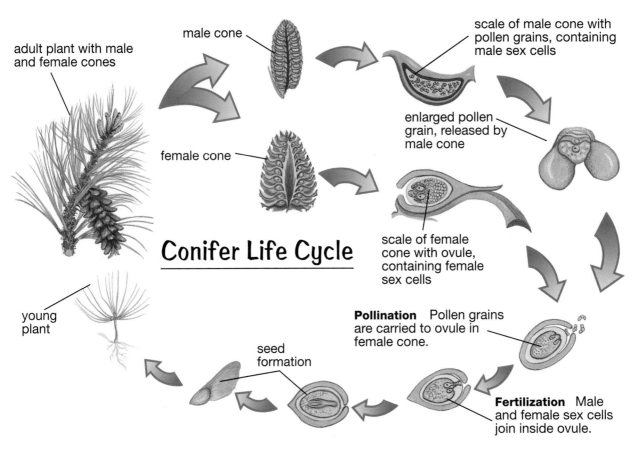

Conifer Life Cycle

adult plant with male and female cones

male cone

scale of male cone with pollen grains, containing male sex cells

enlarged pollen grain, released by male cone

female cone

scale of female cone with ovule, containing female sex cells

young plant

seed formation

Pollination Pollen grains are carried to ovule in female cone.

Fertilization Male and female sex cells join inside ovule.

INVESTIGATION 2 WRAP-UP

THINK IT WRITE IT

REVIEW

1. Describe the four main stages in the growth of a maple seed into an adult tree.

2. Describe how seeds and fruit form in a flower. Identify some inherited traits in plants.

CRITICAL THINKING

3. List two ways in which a female cone is like a flower. List two ways in which it is different.

4. Compare the life cycle of a flowering plant to that of a cone plant.

REFLECT & EVALUATE

Word Power

Write the letter of the term that best completes each sentence. *Not all terms will be used.*

1. The ovary surrounding the seed or seeds develops into a _____.

2. The wormlike stage in the life cycle of an insect is called a _____.

3. A tree that bears cones is a _____.

4. The process that takes place when a male sex cell from a pollen grain joins with a female sex cell inside an ovary is _____.

a. cone
b. conifer
c. fertilization
d. fruit
e. invertebrate
f. larva
g. pollination
h. pupa
i. vertebrate

Check What You Know

Write the term in each pair that best completes each sentence.

1. The stage of metamorphosis at which an insect appears to be at rest but is actually changing is the (larva, pupa) stage.

2. In a human life cycle a person is most likely to have a growth spurt during (adulthood, adolescence).

3. The reproductive organ of a maple tree is the (leaf, flower).

Problem Solving

1. Drawings showing an insect's life cycle are often in the shape of a circle. Explain why.

2. Seeds of flowering plants usually have a hard seed coat and a supply of food. How does this structure help a plant?

3. Make a table that shows how the life cycles of a salmon and a woodpecker are alike and different.

Make a sketch of this flower. On your sketch, label all the numbered parts. Show which part of the flower will grow into the fruit.

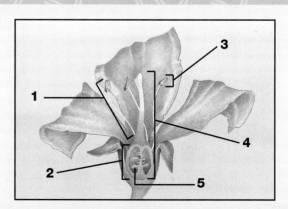

Main Idea and Details

When you read science, it's important to recognize which facts and details support or explain the main idea. First identify the main idea by looking for clues such as a title, or a topic sentence that states the main idea. Then look for statements that support that idea.

> Look for clues to find the main idea.
>
> Look for statements, facts, and details that support the main idea.

Read the paragraph below. Then complete the exercises.

From Flower to Fruit

The flower is the reproductive organ of a flowering plant. Some kinds of plants have flowers that produce both male and female sex cells. Other kinds have flowers that produce either male or female sex cells. When an insect visits a flower, it transfers the male sex cell from one flower to another. This transfer is part of the process of **sexual reproduction** in the flower. During sexual reproduction a male sex cell joins with a female sex cell to produce a fertilized egg. In flowering plants, this fertilized egg develops into a tiny plant enclosed in a seed. Through sexual reproduction, the tiny plant inherits traits, such as petal color and fruit shape, from each parent plant.

1. Write the letter of the sentence that states the main idea of the paragraph.

   a. The flower is the reproductive organ of a flowering plant.

   b. Tiny plants inherit traits, such as petal color and fruit shape, from each parent plant.

   c. Some plants produce both male and female sex cells.

   d. The fertilized egg develops into a tiny plant.

2. What clue helped you find the main idea?

3. List the most important facts and details that support the main idea.

Using Math **Line Graph**

Bamboo is a fast-growing giant grass. The 24-hour growth of a shoot of one species of bamboo is shown on the line graph below.

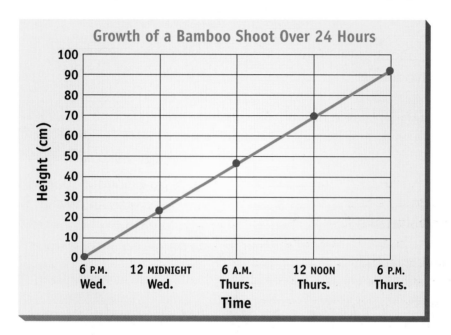

Growth of a Bamboo Shoot Over 24 Hours

Use the information in the graph to complete the exercises that follow.

1. What does the line on the graph represent? Estimate how much the bamboo shoot grows in one hour. Explain.

2. In the line graph above, the line is a straight line. Is the line of every line graph a straight line? Explain.

You may want to use a calculator for Exercises 3 and 4.

3. Some bamboo species can grow to a height of 37 m. If the bamboo shoot shown continued growing at the rate shown, how long would it take to reach a height of 37 m? Round your answer to the nearest whole number.

4. Suppose another species of bamboo grows at one half the rate of the bamboo species shown on the graph. How long would it take a shoot of that species to grow to a height of 10 m? Round your answer to the nearest whole number.

WRAP-UP!

On your own, use scientific methods to investigate a question about systems in living things.

THINK LIKE A SCIENTIST

Ask a Question

Pose a question about plants or animals that you would like to investigate. For example, ask, "How does turning a seedling upside down affect the direction in which its roots grow?"

Make a Hypothesis

Suggest a hypothesis that is a possible answer to the question. One hypothesis is that the roots of a seedling that is turned upside down will curve downward and grow toward the ground.

Plan and Do a Test

Plan a controlled experiment to find the effect that turning a seedling upside down has on the direction in which roots grow. You could start a number of seedlings growing on wet paper towels placed inside sealed clear plastic bags. Develop a procedure that uses these materials to test the hypothesis. With permission, carry out your experiment. Follow the safety guidelines on pages S14–S15.

Record and Analyze

Observe carefully and record your data accurately. Make repeated observations.

Draw Conclusions

Look for evidence to support the hypothesis or to show that it is false. Draw conclusions about the hypothesis. Repeat the experiment to verify the results.

WRITING IN SCIENCE
Letter of Request

Write a letter to request information about lung diseases and their prevention. Use these guidelines to write your letter of request.

- Find the Internet addresses of helpful Web sites that have reliable information.

- Use the parts of a formal letter: heading, inside address, greeting, and closing.

- Clearly state your request.

- Include a self-addressed, stamped envelope.

SCIENCE and MATH TOOLBOX

Using a Microscope

A microscope makes it possible to see very small things by magnifying them. Some microscopes have a set of lenses that magnify objects by different amounts.

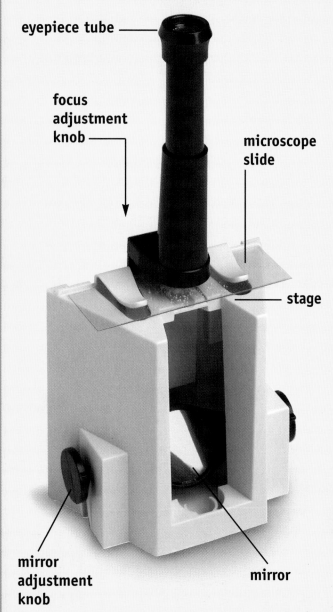

eyepiece tube

focus adjustment knob

microscope slide

stage

mirror adjustment knob

mirror

Examine Some Salt Grains

Handle a microscope carefully; it can break easily. Carry it firmly with both hands and avoid touching the lenses.

1. Turn the mirror toward a source of light. **NEVER** use the Sun as a light source.

2. Place a few grains of salt on the slide. Put the slide on the stage of the microscope.

3. Bring the salt grains into focus. Turn the adjustment knob on the back of the microscope as you look through the eyepiece.

4. Raise the eyepiece tube to increase the magnification; lower it to decrease magnification.

Salt grains magnified one hundred times (100X)

Making a
Bar Graph

A bar graph helps you organize and compare data. For example, you might want to make a bar graph to compare weather data for different places.

Make a Bar Graph of Annual Snowfall

For more than 20 years, the cities listed in the table have been recording their yearly snowfall. The table shows the average number of centimeters of snow that the cities receive each year. Use the data in the table to make a bar graph showing the cities' average annual snowfall.

Snowfall	
City	Snowfall (cm)
Atlanta, GA	5
Charleston, SC	1.5
Houston, TX	1
Jackson, MS	3
New Orleans, LA	0.5
Tucson, AZ	3

1. Title your graph. The title should help a reader understand what your graph describes.

2. Choose a scale and mark equal intervals. The vertical scale should include the least value and the greatest value in the set of data.

3. Label the vertical axis *Snowfall (cm)* and the horizontal axis *City*. Space the city names equally.

4. Carefully graph the data. Depending on the interval you choose, some amounts may be between two numbers.

5. Check each step of your work.

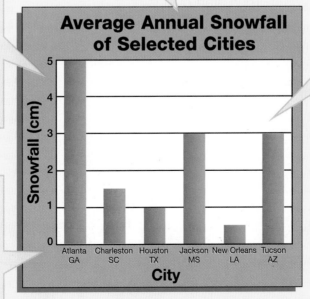

Average Annual Snowfall of Selected Cities

Using a Calculator

After you've made measurements, a calculator can help you analyze your data. Some calculators have a memory key that allows you to save the result of one calculation while you do another.

Add and Divide to Find Percent

The table shows the amount of rain that was collected using a rain gauge in each month of one year. You can use a calculator to help you find the total yearly rainfall. Then you can find the percent of rain that fell during January.

1. Add the numbers. When you add a series of numbers, you need not press the equal sign until the last number is entered. Just press the plus sign after you enter each number (except the last).

2. If you make a mistake while you are entering numbers, press the clear entry (CE/C) key to erase your mistake. Then you can continue entering the rest of the numbers you are adding. If you can't fix your mistake, you can press the (CE/C) key once or twice until the screen shows 0. Then start over.

3. Your total should be 1,131. Now clear the calculator until the screen shows 0. Then divide the rainfall amount for January by the total yearly rainfall (1,131). Press the percent (%) key. Then press the equal sign key.

214 ÷ 1131 % =

The percent of yearly rainfall that fell in January is 18.921309, which rounds to 19%.

Rainfall	
Month	Rain (mm)
Jan.	214
Feb.	138
Mar.	98
Apr.	157
May	84
June	41
July	5
Aug.	23
Sept.	48
Oct.	75
Nov.	140
Dec.	108

clear entry

percent

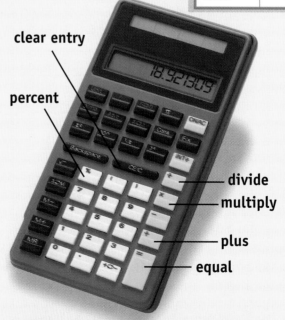

divide

multiply

plus

equal

Finding an Average

An average is a way to describe a set of data using one number. For example, you could compare the surface temperature of several stars that are of the same type. You could find the average surface temperature of these stars.

Add and Divide to Find the Average

Suppose scientists found the surface temperature of eight blue-white stars to be those shown in the table. What is the average surface temperature of the stars listed?

Surface Temperature of Selected Blue-white Stars

Blue-white Star	Surface Temperature (°F)
1	7,200
2	6,100
3	6,000
4	6,550
5	7,350
6	6,800
7	7,500
8	6,300

1. First find the sum of the data. Add the numbers in the list.

```
   7,200
   6,100
   6,000
   6,550
   7,350
   6,800
   7,500
 + 6,300
  ------
  53,800
```

2. Then divide the sum (53,800) by the number of addends (8).

```
        6,725
   8 ) 53,800
      - 48
       ----
        58
       - 56
        ----
         20
        - 16
         ----
          40
         - 40
          ---
           0
```

3. $53,800 \div 8 = 6,725$
The average surface temperature of these eight blue-white stars is 6,725°F.

Using a Tape Measure or Ruler

Tape measures, metersticks, and rulers are tools for measuring length. Scientists use units such as kilometers, meters, centimeters, and millimeters when making length measurements.

Use a Meterstick

1. Work with a partner to find the height of your reach. Stand facing a chalkboard. Reach up as high as you can with one hand.

2. Have your partner use chalk to mark the chalkboard at the highest point of your reach.

3. Use a meterstick to measure your reach to the nearest centimeter. Measure from the floor to the chalk mark. Record the height of your reach.

Use a Tape Measure

1. Use a tape measure to find the circumference of, or distance around, your partner's head. Wrap the tape around your partner's head.

2. Find the line where the tape begins to wrap over itself.

3. Record the distance around your partner's head to the nearest millimeter.

Measuring Volume

A graduated cylinder, a measuring cup, and a beaker are used to measure volume. Volume is the amount of space something takes up. Most of the containers that scientists use to measure volume have a scale marked in milliliters (mL).

Measure the Volume of a Liquid

1. Measure the volume of some juice. Pour the juice into a measuring container.

2. Move your head so that your eyes are level with the top of the juice. Read the scale line that is closest to the surface of the juice. If the surface of the juice is curved up on the sides, look at the lowest point of the curve.

3. Read the measurement on the scale. You can estimate the value between two lines on the scale to obtain a more accurate measurement.

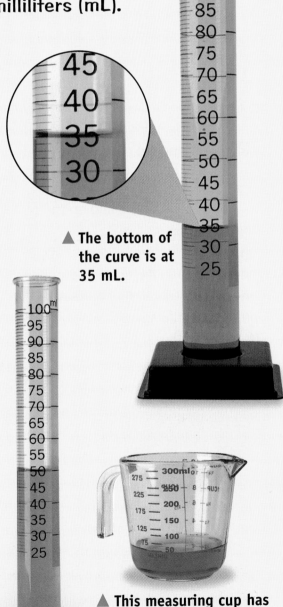

▲ The bottom of the curve is at 35 mL.

This beaker has marks for each 25 mL. ▶

This graduated cylinder has marks for every 1 mL. ▶

▲ This measuring cup has marks for each 25 mL.

Using a Thermometer

A thermometer is used to measure temperature. When the liquid in the tube of a thermometer gets warmer, it expands and moves farther up the tube. Different scales can be used to measure temperature, but scientists usually use the Celsius scale.

Measure the Temperature of a Cold Liquid

1. Half fill a cup with chilled liquid.

2. Hold the thermometer so that the bulb is in the center of the liquid. Be sure that there are no bright lights or direct sunlight shining on the bulb.

3. Wait until you see the liquid in the tube of the thermometer stop moving. Read the scale line that is closest to the top of the liquid in the tube. The thermometer shown reads 21°C (about 70°F).

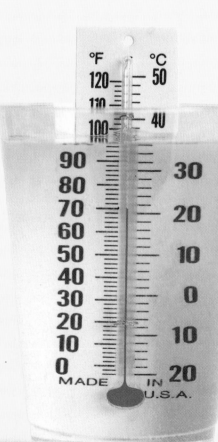

Using a
Balance

A balance is used to measure mass. Mass is the amount of matter in an object. To find the mass of an object, place the object in the left pan of the balance. Place standard masses in the right pan.

Measure the Mass of a Ball

1. Check that the empty pans are balanced, or level with each other. The pointer at the base should be on the middle mark. If it needs to be adjusted, move the slider on the back of the balance a little to the left or right.

2. Place a ball on the left pan. Notice that the pointer moves and that the pans are no longer level with each other. Then add standard masses, one

at a time, to the right pan. When the pointer is at the middle mark again, the pans are balanced. Each pan is holding the same amount of matter, and the same mass.

3. Each standard mass is marked to show its number of grams. Add the number of grams marked on the masses in the pan. The total is the mass of the ball in grams.

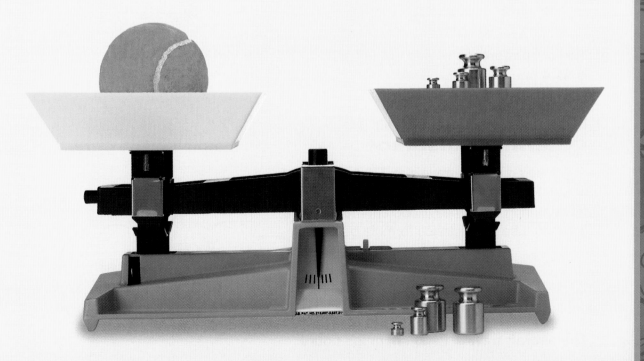

Using an Equation or Formula

Equations and formulas can help you to determine measurements that are not easily made.

Use the Diameter of a Circle to Find Its Circumference

Find the circumference of a circle that has a diameter of 10 cm. To determine the circumference of a circle, use the formula below.

$$C = \pi d$$

$$C = 3.14 \times 10$$

$$C = 31.4 \text{ cm}$$

π is the symbol for pi. Always use 3.14 as the value for π, unless another value for pi is given.

The circumference of this circle is 31.4 cm.

The circumference (*C*) is a measure of the distance around a circle.

10 cm

The diameter (*d*) of a circle is a line segment that passes through the center of the circle and connects two points on the circle.

Use Rate and Time to Determine Distance

Suppose an aircraft travels at 772 km/h for 2.5 hours. How many kilometers does the aircraft travel during that time? To determine distance traveled, use the distance formula below.

$$d = rt$$

$$d = 772 \times 2.5$$

$$d = 1{,}930 \text{ km}$$

d = distance

r = rate, or the speed at which the aircraft is traveling.

t = the length of time traveled

The aircraft travels 1,930 km in 2.5 hours.

Making a Chart to Organize Data

A chart can help you record, compare, or classify information.

Organize Properties of Elements

Suppose you collected the data shown at the right. The data presents properties of silver, gold, lead, and iron.

You could organize this information in a chart by classifying the physical properties of each element.

My Data

Silver (Ag) has a density of 10.5 g/cm³. It melts at 961°C and boils at 2,212°C. It is used in dentistry and to make jewelry and electronic conductors.

Gold melts at 1,064°C and boils at 2,966°C. Its chemical symbol is Au. It has a density of 19.3 g/cm³ and is used for jewelry, in coins, and in dentistry.

The melting point of lead (Pb) is 328°C. The boiling point is 1,740°C. It has a density of 11.3 g/cm³. Some uses for lead are in storage batteries, paints, and dyes.

Iron (Fe) has a density of 7.9 g/cm³. It will melt at 1,535°C and boil at 3,000°C. It is used for building materials, in manufacturing, and as a dietary supplement.

Create categories that describe the information you have found.

Give the chart a title that describes what is listed in it.

Properties of Some Elements

Element	Symbol	Density g/cm³	Melting Point (°C)	Boiling Point (°C)	Some Uses
Silver	Ag	10.5	961	2,212	jewelry, dentistry, electric conductors
Gold	Au	19.3	1,064	2,966	jewelry, dentistry, coins
Lead	Pb	11.3	328	1,740	storage batteries, paints, dyes
Iron	Fe	7.9	1,535	3,000	building materials, manufacturing, dietary supplement

Make sure the information is listed accurately in each column.

Reading a Circle Graph

A circle graph shows the whole divided into parts. You can use a circle graph to compare parts to each other or to compare parts to the whole.

Read a Circle Graph of Land Area

The whole circle represents the approximate land area of all of the continents on Earth. The number on each wedge indicates the land area of each continent. From the graph you can determine that altogether the land area of the continents is 148,000,000 square kilometers.

Together Antarctica and Australia are about equal to the land area of North America.

Africa accounts for more of the Earth's land area than South America.

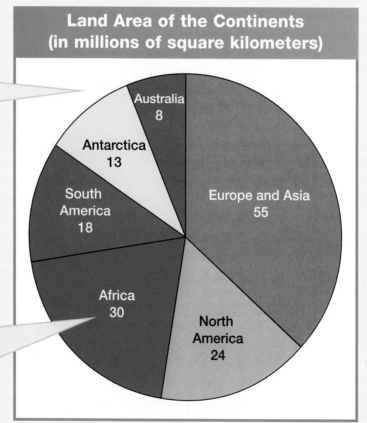

Land Area of the Continents (in millions of square kilometers)

Australia 8

Antarctica 13

South America 18

Europe and Asia 55

Africa 30

North America 24

Making a
Line Graph

A line graph is a way to show continuous change over time. You can use the information from a table to make a line graph.

Dallas–Fort Worth Airport Temperature

Hour	Temp. (°C)
6 A.M.	22
7 A.M.	24
8 A.M.	25
9 A.M.	26
10 A.M.	27
11 A.M.	29
12 NOON	31
1 P.M.	32
2 P.M.	33
3 P.M.	34
4 P.M.	35
5 P.M.	35
6 P.M.	34

Make a Line Graph of Temperatures

The table shows temperature readings over a 12-hour period at the Dallas–Fort Worth Airport in Texas. This data can also be displayed in a line graph that shows temperature change over time.

1. Choose a title. The title should help a reader understand what your graph describes.

2. Choose a scale and mark equal intervals. The vertical scale should include the least value and the greatest value in the set of data.

3. Label the horizontal axis *Time* and the vertical axis *Temperature (°C)*.

4. Write the hours on the horizontal axis. Space the hours equally.

5. Carefully graph the data. Depending on the interval you choose, some temperatures will be between two numbers.

6. Check each step of your work.

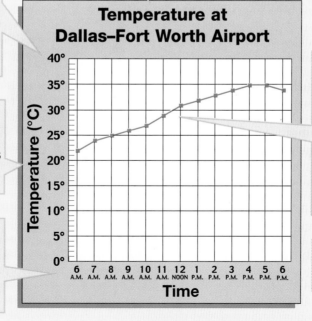

Temperature at Dallas–Fort Worth Airport

Measuring
Elapsed Time

Sometimes you may need to find out how much time has passed, or elapsed. A clock is often used to find elapsed time. You can also change units and add or subtract to find out how much time has passed.

Using a Clock to Find Elapsed Minutes

You need to time an experiment for 20 minutes. It is 1:30.

Minutes

Start at 1:30. Count ahead 20 minutes, by fives to 1:50. Stop the experiment at 1:50.

Using a Clock or Stopwatch to Find Elapsed Seconds

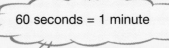

60 seconds = 1 minute

You need to time an experiment for 15 seconds. You can use a second hand on a clock. You can also use a stopwatch to figure out elapsed seconds.

Seconds

Wait until the second hand is on a number. Then start the experiment.

Stop the experiment when 15 seconds have passed.

Press the reset button on the stopwatch so you see 0:00₀₀.

Press the start button to begin.

When you see 0:15₀₀, press the stop button on the watch.

Changing Units and Then Adding or Subtracting to Find Elapsed Time

If you know how to change units of time, you can use addition and subtraction to find elapsed time.

To change from a larger unit to a smaller unit, multiply.

$$2 \text{ d} = \blacksquare \text{ h}$$
$$2 \times 24 = 48$$
$$2 \text{ d} = 48 \text{ h}$$

Units of Time

60 seconds (s) = 1 minute (min)

60 minutes = 1 hour (h)

24 hours = 1 day (d)

7 days = 1 week (wk)

52 weeks = 1 year (yr)

To change from a smaller unit to a larger unit, divide.

$$78 \text{ wk} = \blacksquare \text{ yr}$$
$$78 \div 52 = 1\tfrac{1}{2}$$
$$78 \text{ wk} = 1\tfrac{1}{2} \text{ yr}$$

Another Example

Suppose it took juice in an ice-pop mold from 6:40 A.M. until 10:15 A.M. to freeze. How long did it take for the juice to freeze? To find out, subtract.

$$
\begin{array}{cc}
9 \text{ h} & 75 \text{ min} \\
\cancel{10 \text{ h}} & \cancel{15 \text{ min}} \\
- \quad 6 \text{ h} & 40 \text{ min} \\
\hline
3 \text{ h} & 35 \text{ min}
\end{array}
$$

Rename 10 h 15 min as 9 h 75 min, since 1 h = 60 min.

You can also add to find elapsed time.

$$
\begin{array}{cccc}
& 3 \text{ h} & 30 \text{ min} & 14 \text{ s} \\
+ & 1 \text{ h} & 40 \text{ min} & 45 \text{ s} \\
\hline
& 4 \text{ h} & 70 \text{ min} & 59 \text{ s} = 5 \text{ h} \ 10 \text{ min} \ 59 \text{ s}
\end{array}
$$

MEASUREMENTS

Volume
1 L of sports drink is a little more than 1 qt.

Area
A basketball court covers about 4,700 ft^2. It covers about 435 m^2.

Mass and Weight
A basketball has a mass of about 650 g. It weighs about $1\frac{1}{2}$ lb.

Metric Measures

Temperature
Ice melts at 0 degrees Celsius (°C)

Water freezes at 0°C

Water boils at 100°C

Length and Distance
1,000 meters (m) = 1 kilometer (km)

100 centimeters (cm) = 1 m

10 millimeters (mm) = 1 cm

Force
1 newton (N) =
    1 kilogram x meter/second/second
    (kg x m/s^2)

Volume
1 cubic meter (m^3) = 1 m x 1 m x 1 m

1 cubic centimeter (cm^3) =
    1 cm x 1 cm x 1 cm

1 liter (L) = 1,000 milliliters (mL)

1 cm^3 = 1 mL

Area
1 square kilometer (km^2) = 1 km x 1 km

1 hectare = 10,000 m^2

Mass
1,000 grams (g) = 1 kilogram (kg)

1,000 milligrams (mg) = 1 g

Temperature

The temperature at an indoor basketball game might be 25°C, which is 77°F.

Length/ Distance

A basketball rim is about 10 ft high, or a little more than 3 m from the floor.

Customary Measures

Temperature

Ice melts at 32 degrees Fahrenheit (°F)

Water freezes at 32°F

Water boils at 212°F

Length and Distance

12 inches (in.) = 1 foot (ft)

3 ft = 1 yard (yd)

5,280 ft = 1 mile (mi)

Weight

16 ounces (oz) = 1 pound (lb)

2,000 pounds = 1 ton (T)

Volume of Fluids

8 fluid ounces (fl oz) = 1 cup (c)

2 c = 1 pint (pt)

2 pt = 1 quart (qt)

4 qt = 1 gallon (gal)

Metric and Customary Rates

km/h = kilometers per hour

m/s = meters per second

mph = miles per hour

GLOSSARY

Pronunciation Key

Symbol	Key Words	Symbol	Key Words
a	cat	g	get
ā	ape	h	help
ä	cot, car	j	jump
		k	kiss, call
e	ten, berry	l	leg
ē	me	m	meat
		n	nose
i	fit, here	p	put
ī	ice, fire	r	red
		s	see
ō	go	t	top
ô	fall, for	v	vat
oi	oil	w	wish
oo	look, pull	y	yard
o͞o	tool, rule	z	zebra
ou	out, crowd		
		ch	chin, arch
u	up	ŋ	ring, drink
ʉ	fur, shirt	sh	she, push
		th	thin, truth
ə	a in ago	*th*	then, father
	e in agent	zh	measure
	i in pencil		
	o in atom	
	u in circus	
b	bed	
d	dog	
f	fall	

A heavy stress mark (′) is placed after a syllable that gets a heavy, or primary, stress, as in **picture** (pik′chər).

absolute age (ab'sə loot āj) The actual age of an object. (E77) The *absolute age* of this rock is 3,500 years.

absolute magnitude (ab'sə loot mag'nə tood) The measure of a star's brightness, based on the amount of light it actually gives off. (B61) The Sun's *absolute magnitude* is less than that of many other stars.

adaptation (ad əp tā'shən) A structure or behavior that enables an organism to survive in its environment. (D9) The thick fur of some animals is an *adaptation* to cold environments.

adult (ə dult') The final stage of an organism's life cycle. (A74) A butterfly is the *adult* form of a caterpillar.

air sacs (er saks) Thin-walled chambers in the lung through which oxygen moves into the blood. (A49) Each lung contains millions of *air sacs*.

alloy (al'oi) A solution of two or more metals, which has properties of its own. (C30) Pewter is an *alloy* of tin and other metals such as copper and lead.

amplitude (am'plə tood) The height of a wave from its resting position to its highest or lowest point; a measure of the amount of energy in a sound wave. (F17, F55) The *amplitude* of a loud sound is greater than the amplitude of a soft sound.

anticline (an'ti klīn) An upward fold of rock layers. (E82) Bending layers of rock formed an *anticline*.

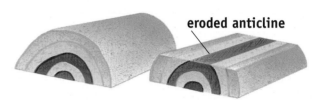

eroded anticline

apparent magnitude (ə per'ənt mag'nə tood) The measure of a star's brightness as seen from Earth. (B60) A star's *apparent magnitude* depends on the amount of light it gives off and on its distance from Earth.

arteries (art'ər ēz) Blood vessels that carry blood away from the heart. (A57) *Arteries* have thick, muscular walls.

atom (at'əm) The smallest particle of an element that has the properties of that element. (C22) Water is a combination of one *atom* of oxygen with two of hydrogen.

audiocassette (ô'dē ō kə set) A small container holding magnetic tape that is used for playing or recording sound. (F89) We inserted an *audiocassette* into the tape recorder.

auditory nerve (ô'də tôr ē nʉrv) A nerve in the ear that carries nerve impulses to the brain. (F83) A damaged *auditory nerve* will affect hearing.

axis (ak'sis) The imaginary line on which an object rotates. (B13) Earth's *axis* runs between the North and South Poles.

B

big-bang theory (big′ baŋ thē′ə rē)
A hypothesis, supported by data, that
describes how the universe began with
a huge explosion. (B39) The *big-bang
theory* holds that everything in the universe was once concentrated at one tiny
point.

biodiversity (bī ō də vʉr′sə tē) The
variety of organisms that live in Earth's
many ecosystems; the variety of plants
and animals that live within a particular
ecosystem. (D56) The *biodiversity* of
an ecosystem quickly changes after a
natural disaster.

biome (bī′ōm) A major land ecosystem having a distinct combination
of plants and animals. (D46) Some
biomes, such as the tundra, do not
easily support human populations.

black dwarf (blak dwarf) The cool,
dark body that is the final stage in the life
cycle of a low-mass star. (B65) When the
Sun dies, it will become a *black dwarf.*

black hole (blak hôl) An extremely
dense, invisible object in space whose
gravity is so great that not even light
can escape it. (B67) Scientists think
that the remains of a very massive star
can collapse following a supernova
explosion to form a *black hole.*

blood (blud) A tissue made up of a
liquid called plasma and several types
of cells. (A56) *Blood* carries oxygen
and nutrients to body cells.

bronchial tubes (brän′kē əl tōōbz)
Tubes that carry air from the trachea to
the lungs. (A48) Air flows to and from
the lungs through the *bronchial tubes.*

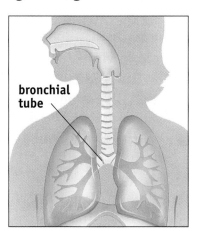

bronchial
tube

C

capillaries (kap′ə ler ēz) Tiny blood
vessels that connect the smallest arteries with the smallest veins. (A57)
Nutrients pass through the walls of the
capillaries into the cells.

carbon dioxide–oxygen cycle
(kär′bən dī äks′īd äks′i jen sī′kəl)
A natural cycle in which plants and
other producers use carbon dioxide and
produce oxygen, and animals, plants,
and other living things use oxygen and
produce carbon dioxide. (D32) The *carbon dioxide–oxygen cycle* must be
duplicated in space if humans wish to
make long voyages to other planets.

carnivore (kär′nə vôr) A consumer
that eats only other animals. (D16)
Lions are *carnivores* that prey on
zebras and other large plant-eaters.

cell (sel) The basic unit of structure of all living things. (A11) Even though plant *cells* can be different sizes, they still have many of the same structures.

cell membrane (sel mem′brān) A thin layer that surrounds all cells and allows water and dissolved materials to pass into and out of the cell. (A13) In plant cells, the *cell membrane* lies inside the cell wall.

cell respiration (sel res pə rā′shən) The process of using oxygen to release energy from food. (A23, D32) Animals and plants release carbon dioxide as a waste product of *cell respiration.*

cell wall (sel wôl) The tough outer covering of a plant cell that gives the cell its rigid shape. (A13) A *cell wall* is not found in animal cells.

cementation (sē men tā′shən) A process in which minerals, deposited as water evaporates, bind sediments into solid rock. (E44) Sandstone is a sedimentary rock formed by *cementation.*

chemical change (kem′i kəl chānj) A change in which one or more new substances form. (C58) The rusting of an iron nail is an example of a *chemical change.*

chemical formula (kem′i kəl fôr′myōō lə) A group of symbols that shows the elements that make up a compound. (C26) The *chemical formula* for water is H_2O.

chemical property (kem′i kəl präp′ər tē) A description of how a kind of matter can change into other kinds of matter. (C14) The ability to burn is a *chemical property* of kerosene.

chemical symbol (kem′i kəl sim′bəl) A shorthand way to represent the name of an element. (C23) The *chemical symbol* for iron is Fe.

chloroplast (klôr′ə plast) A structure in plant cells that captures light energy that is used in the food-making process. (A13) *Chloroplasts* are located within cells in the leaves of a plant.

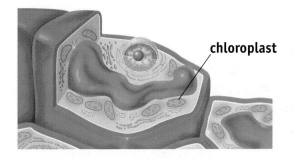

chloroplast

circulatory system (sur′kyōō lə tôr ē sis′təm) The transport system of the body that carries oxygen and nutrients to all cells and then removes wastes. (A56) The *circulatory system* brings nutrients and oxygen to the cells.

cleavage (klēv′ij) The tendency of some minerals to split along flat surfaces. (E15) Salt, or halite, shows *cleavage* in three planes.

coastal ocean (kōs′təl ō′shən) A saltwater ecosystem close to the shoreline that supports an abundance of life. (D52) The *coastal ocean* is an ecosystem that lies beyond the shoreline.

comet (käm′it) A small object in space, made of ice, dust, gas, and rock, that orbits a star and that can form a gaseous tail. (B24) A *comet* begins to melt as it approaches the Sun.

commensalism (kə men′səl iz əm) A close relationship between two kinds of organisms that benefits one of the organisms while neither benefiting nor hurting the other. (D20) The way that some insects use their resemblance to plants to hide from predators is an example of *commensalism*.

community (kə myōō′nə tē) All the organisms living together in a particular *ecosystem*. (D8) Raccoons, deer, and trees are part of a forest *community*.

compact disc (käm′pakt disk) A small disk on which sounds are digitally recorded and played back when read by a laser beam. (F90) This *compact disc*, or CD, plays for one hour.

complete metamorphosis (kəm-plēt′ met ə môr′fə sis) The development of an organism through four stages—egg, larva, pupa, and adult. (A74) The life cycle of a butterfly is an example of *complete metamorphosis*.

compound (käm′pound) A substance made up of two or more elements that are chemically joined, or linked. (C26) Water, made of the elements hydrogen and oxygen, is an example of a *compound*.

compound microscope (käm′pound mī′krə skōp) A viewing instrument that uses two lenses to magnify objects many times. (F41) The human hair appeared 1,000 times larger than actual size under the *compound microscope*.

compression (kəm presh′ən) A region in a sound wave where particles have been pushed together. (F55) The *compressions* produced by a vibrating tuning fork are areas of greater-than-normal air pressure.

concave lens (kän′kāv lenz) A lens that is thicker at the edges than it is in the middle and that causes light rays to spread apart. (F32) A *concave lens* is used to correct nearsightedness.

concave mirror (kän′kāv mir′ər) A mirror that curves inward at the middle. (F23) A *concave mirror* is used in a reflecting telescope.

concrete (kän′krēt) A mixture of rock material and cement that is used as a building material. (E24) This sidewalk is made of *concrete*.

condensation (kän dən sā′shən) The process by which a gas changes to a liquid. (C56, D34) *Condensation* can occur on a glass containing ice cubes as the gas water vapor changes to liquid water.

conduction (kən duk′shən) The transfer of heat energy by direct contact between particles. (C40) Heat travels through a metal by *conduction*.

conifer (kän'ə fər) A tree or shrub that bears its seeds in cones. (A91) The cones of each species of *conifer* are distinct and different from each other.

constellation (kän stə lā'shən) A group of stars that form a fixed pattern in the night sky. (B10) The *constellation* known as the Little Dipper contains the North Star.

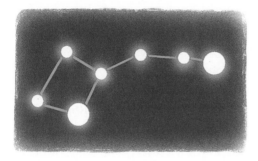

consumer (kən soom'ər) A living thing that obtains energy by eating other living things. (D16) Meat eaters and plant eaters are *consumers*.

contact lens (kän'takt lenz) A thin lens worn over the cornea of the eye, usually to correct vision problems. (F35) Some people use *contact lenses* rather than eyeglasses to improve their vision.

controlled experiment (kən trōld' ek sper'ə mənt) A test of a hypothesis in which the setups are identical in all ways except one. (S7) In the controlled experiment, one beaker of water contained salt.

convection (kən vek'shən) The transfer of heat energy through liquids and gases by moving particles. (C41) When a pot of water is placed on a heat source, the heat is carried throughout the water by *convection*.

convex lens (kän'veks lenz) A lens that is thicker in the middle than at the edges and that brings light rays together. (F32) A *convex lens* is used to correct farsightedness.

convex mirror (kän'veks mir'ər) A mirror that curves outward at the middle. (F23) The side-view mirror of a car is a *convex mirror*.

core (kôr) The innermost layer of Earth, which consists of a molten outer part and a solid inner part. (E69) Temperatures inside the *core* of Earth are nearly as hot as those on the Sun's surface.

crest (krest) The highest point of a wave; in a sound wave, the regions of lower air pressure. (F17, F55) The top of a wave is its *crest*.

crust (krust) The outer layer of Earth. (E68) Earth's *crust* is a thin layer of rock.

cytoplasm (sīt'ō plaz əm) The jelly-like substance that fills much of the cell. (A13) The nucleus, vacuoles, and many other cell structures float in the *cytoplasm*.

decibel (des'ə bəl) A unit used to measure the loudness or intensity of sound. (F77) Sounds that have an intensity greater than 120 *decibels* (db) can hurt your ears.

decomposer (dē kəm pōz′ər) A living thing that breaks down the remains of dead organisms. (D16) *Decomposers*, such as fungi, get their energy from the remains of dead plants they break down.

deciduous forest (dē sij′o͞o əs fôr′ist) A biome that contains many trees and in which rainfall is moderate. (D49) *Deciduous forests* support a great variety of animal life.

desert (dez′ərt) A biome in which plant life is not abundant and rainfall is low. (D48) Plants that live in a *desert* have adaptations to conserve water.

diaphragm (dī′ə fram) The dome-shaped muscle that separates the chest from the stomach area. (A46) When you breathe in, the *diaphragm* moves down, and air rushes into the lungs.

digestive system (di jes′tiv sis′təm) The organ system in which food is broken down into a form that body cells can use. (A38) Many medicines treat disorders of the *digestive system*.

donor (dō′nər) A person who gives blood for a blood transfusion. (A58) Blood banks depend on *donors* to provide blood for transfusions.

ecosystem (ek′ō sis təm) An area in which living and nonliving things interact. (D8) An oak tree and the organisms that inhabit it can be thought of as a small *ecosystem*.

egg (eg) The first stage in an organism's life cycle. (A74) A baby bird hatches from an *egg*.

electromagnetic radiation (ē lektrō mag net′ik rā dē ā′shən) Wave energy given off by the Sun and some other objects. (F8) Visible light is a form of *electromagnetic radiation*.

electron microscope (ē lek′trän mī′krə skōp) A viewing instrument that magnifies objects thousands of times by using a beam of electrons instead of a beam of light. (F42) Doctors studied the virus through an *electron microscope*.

element (el′ə mənt) A basic kind of matter made up of just one kind of atom. (C22) Iron and oxygen are *elements*.

embryo (em′brē ō) An organism in its earliest stages of development; in most plants it is found inside a seed. (A85) When conditions for growth are suitable, the *embryo* inside the seed develops into a young plant.

endangered (en dān′jərd) In danger of becoming extinct. (D59) As the destruction of the Amazon rain forest continues, the number of *endangered* species increases.

energy (en′ər jə) The ability to cause change. (C11, F8) *Energy* from the Sun warms the air.

enzymes (en′zīmz) Chemicals that help break down food. (A39) Digestive *enzymes* in the stomach break down food into smaller particles.

erosion (ē rō′zhən) The breaking down and carrying away of rock and soil caused by such forces as wind and flowing water. (E82) The pounding waves caused *erosion* of the sandy shoreline.

esophagus (i säf′ə gəs) The muscular tube that connects the mouth to the stomach. (A40) After food is swallowed, it travels through the *esophagus* to the stomach.

eustachian tube (yōō stā′kē ən tōōb) A tube that connects the throat and the middle ear. (F83) The *eustachian tube* equalizes the air pressure on both sides of the eardrum.

evaporation (ē vap ə rā′shən) The process by which liquid water changes to water vapor. (C56, D34) One phase of the water cycle is the *evaporation* of water from lakes, rivers, and oceans.

excretory system (eks′krə tôrē sis′təm) The system for ridding the body of harmful wastes produced by the cells. (A62) The kidneys, lungs, and skin are all organs of the *excretory system*.

extinct (ek stiŋkt′) No longer living as a species. (D59) The passenger pigeon is an *extinct* species.

passenger pigeon

extraterrestrial (eks trə tə res′trē əl) A being from outer space; any object from beyond Earth. (B88) It would be extraordinary for scientists to discover that there is *extraterrestrial* life.

fault (fôlt) A break in rock along which rocks have moved. (E89) Forces within Earth's crust produce *faults*.

fertilization (furt′′l ə zā′shən) The process by which a male sex cell joins with a female sex cell. In flowering plants, fertilization takes place in the pistil. (A85) *Fertilization* occurs after a pollen tube reaches the ovary.

filter (fil′tər) A device that lets certain colors of light pass through while absorbing others. (F47) The stage manager placed a red *filter* over the spotlight.

focal point (fō′kəl point) The point at which light rays passing through a lens come together. (F32) Rays of light meet at the *focal point*.

fold (fōld) A bend in a layer of rock. (E81) Forces within Earth can cause a *fold* to form in rock layers.

food chain (fōōd chān) The path of energy transfer from one living organism to another in an ecosystem. (D27) Energy moves from producers to consumers in a *food chain*.

food web (food web) The overlapping food chains that link producers, consumers, and decomposers in an ecosystem. (D28) Some consumers in a *food web* eat both plants and animals.

fossil (fäs'əl) The remains or traces of a living thing from the past, preserved in rock. (E46) *Fossils* can include imprints of animal skeletons pressed into rock.

free fall (frē fôl) The motion of a freely falling object, such as that of a spacecraft in orbit around Earth. (B79) Astronauts experiencing *free fall* in space feel weightless.

frequency (frē'kwən sē) The number of waves produced in a unit of time, such as a second. (F18, F55) The *frequency* of light waves varies with the color of the light.

fruit (frōōt) The enlarged ovary of a flower that protects the developing seeds. (A85) Some *fruits*, such as peaches or mangoes, contain only one seed.

galaxy (gal'ək sē) A vast group of billions of stars that are held together by gravity. (B70) The Milky Way is a typical spiral *galaxy*.

gas (gas) Matter that does not have a definite shape or volume. (C21) Helium is a light *gas* that is sometimes used to fill balloons.

gas giant (gas jī'ənt) A large planet that is made up mostly of gaseous and liquid substances, with little or no solid surface. (B47) Jupiter is a *gas giant.*

geocentric model (jē ō sen'trik mäd''l) A representation of the universe in which stars and planets revolve around Earth. (B37) Ptolemy proposed a *geocentric model* of the universe.

germination (jʉr mə nā' shən) The sprouting of a seed. (A86) After *germination*, an acorn begins to form a seedling, or tiny young plant.

grassland (gras'land) A biome containing many grasses but few trees and having low to moderate rainfall. (D48) Taller grasses occur in *grasslands* that have more abundant rainfall.

hardness (härd'nis) A measure of how easily a mineral can be scratched. (E13) The *hardness* of diamond is greater than that of any other mineral.

heart (härt) The pump that pushes blood throughout the entire circulatory system. (A56) The human *heart* normally beats about 70 to 80 times per minute.

heliocentric model (hē lē ō sen'trik mäd''l) A representation of the relationship between the Sun and planets in which the planets revolve around the Sun. (B37) Copernicus hypothesized a *heliocentric model* of the solar system.

herbivore (hʉr'bə vôr) A consumer that eats only plants or other producers. (D16) Pandas are *herbivores* that have a very limited diet because they only eat bamboo.

hertz (herts) A unit used to measure wave frequency. (F18, F66) If 100 waves are produced per second, their frequency is 100 *hertz*.

hypothesis (hī päth'ə sis) An idea about or explanation of how or why something happens. (S6) The *hypothesis* about the expanding universe has been supported by evidence gathered by astronomers.

igneous rock (ig'nē əs räk) A type of rock that forms from melted rock that cools and hardens. (E40) Obsidian is an *igneous rock* that forms when lava cools quickly.

index fossil (in'deks fäs'əl) A fossil used to determine the relative age of rock. (E76) The remains of a living thing that lived only at a certain time in the past makes a good *index fossil*.

intensity (in ten'sə tē) A measure of the amount of energy in a sound wave. (F76) A sound that has high *intensity* is loud enough to be heard from a distance.

Internet (in'tər net) A system of interconnected computer networks. (F91) Telephone lines link computer users with the *Internet*.

joule (jo͞ol) The basic unit of energy and of work. (C47) Scientists measure amounts of energy in *joules*.

kidneys (kid'nēz) A pair of organs that clean and filter the blood. (A63) The *kidneys* help remove excess water and salts from the blood.

kinetic energy (ki net'ik en'ər jē) The energy that something has because of its motion. (C48) As a boulder rolls down a steep hill, it gains *kinetic energy*.

lake (lāk) A freshwater ecosystem characterized by still water. (D51) *Lakes* support fish, birds, algae, and other forms of life.

large intestine (lärj in tes'tən) The organ that absorbs water and salts from undigested material. (A43) The major job of the *large intestine* is to absorb water from wastes and return it to the bloodstream.

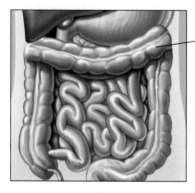

large intestine

larva (lär'və) The wormlike, or grub, stage that follows the egg stage of an insect's life cycle. (A74) The caterpillar is the *larva* stage in the life cycle of a butterfly.

larynx (lar'iŋks) The part of the throat that is used in speaking. (A48) The *larynx* is another name for the voice box.

lava (lä'və) Melted rock material that reaches Earth's surface before it cools and hardens. (E41) A volcano carries *lava* to Earth's surface.

leaf (lēf) A plant part in which photosynthesis takes place. (A19) In a plant such as cabbage, it is the *leaf* that people eat.

lens (lenz) A piece of glass or other transparent material with at least one curved surface that brings together or spreads apart light rays passing through it. (F32) The *lens* in a camera focuses an image on the film.

life processes (līf prä'ses ēz) The functions that a living thing must carry out to stay alive and produce more of its own kind. (A11) Digestion is one of the essential *life processes*.

light-year (līt yir) A unit of measurement representing the distance that light travels in one year. (B61) The distance to stars is measured in *light-years*.

liquid (lik'wid) Matter that has a definite volume but no definite shape. (C21) Water is the most abundant *liquid* on Earth.

luster (lus'tər) The way that the surface of a mineral looks when it reflects light. (E13) Silver and gold have a shiny, metallic *luster*.

magma (mag'mə) Melted rock material that forms deep within Earth. (E40) Some igneous rocks, such as granite, form from *magma*.

mantle (man'təl) A thick layer of rock between the crust and the core of Earth. (E69) The top of the *mantle* is solid rock, but below that is a section of rock that can flow.

mass (mas) A measure of how much matter there is in an object. (C10) A large rock has more *mass* than a pebble.

matter (mat'ər) Anything that has mass and takes up space. (C10) Coal, water, and air are three kinds of *matter*.

melting (melt′iŋ) The change of state from a solid to a liquid. (C56) The process of *melting* changes ice from a solid to liquid water.

metamorphic rock (met ə môr′fik räk) A type of rock that forms from existing rocks because of changes caused by heat, pressure, or chemicals. (E47) Slate is a *metamorphic rock* that forms from the sedimentary rock shale.

meteor (mēt′ē ər) A piece of rock or metal from space that enters Earth's atmosphere. (B25) A *meteor* appears as a streak of light, which is why it is also called a shooting star.

meteorite (mēt′ē ər īt) The remaining material of a meteor that has landed on the ground. (B25) In 1902, scientists were able to examine the largest *meteorite* ever known to land in the United States.

microgravity (mī kro grav′i tē) The condition of very low gravity. (B84) Astronauts experience *microgravity* aboard the space shuttle.

Milky Way Galaxy (milk′ē wā gal′ək sē) A gigantic cluster of billions of stars that is home to our solar system. (B70) The Sun is located in one of the arms of the *Milky Way Galaxy*.

mineral (min′ər əl) A solid element or compound from Earth's crust that has a definite chemical composition and crystal structure. (E12) Quartz is a *mineral*.

mixture (miks′chər) Matter made up of two or more substances. (C27) Air is a *mixture* of many gases, including oxygen, carbon dioxide, and nitrogen.

model (mäd′′l) Something used or made to represent an object or an idea. (E68) Layers of clay can be used as a *model* of layers of rock.

molecule (mäl′i kyo͞ol) A particle made up of two or more atoms, which may be alike or different. (C57) A *molecule* of water contains two hydrogen atoms and one oxygen atom.

moon (mo͞on) A natural object that revolves around a planet. (B44) The planet Mars has two known *moons*.

mutualism (myo͞o′cho͞o əl iz əm) A close relationship between two or more organisms in which all organisms ben-efit. (D20) Bees carrying pollen from flower to flower as they obtain nectar is an example of *mutualism*.

natural resource (nach′ər əl rē′sôrs) Any useful material or energy source found in nature. (E31) *Natural resources* include water, minerals, oil, and coal.

nebula (neb′yə lə) A huge cloud of gas and dust found in space. (B64) A *nebula* can form when a supernova explodes.

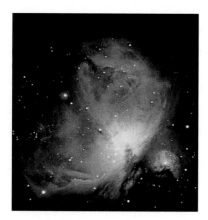

neutron star (n$\overline{oo}$′trän stär) The remains of a massive star that has exploded in a supernova. (B67) A typical *neutron star* is less than 20 km in diameter.

niche (nich) The role that each species plays in a community. (D9) Bees have an important *niche* in pollinating flowers as they gather nectar to make honey.

nitrogen cycle (nī′trə jən sī′kəl) The cycle through which nitrogen changes into compounds that can be used by living things and then returns to the atmosphere. (D40) The *nitrogen cycle* is important to all life forms because nitrogen is needed to make protein.

noise pollution (noiz pə l$\overline{oo}$′shən) The occurrence of loud or unpleasant sound in the environment. (F78) The sounds of city traffic are a form of *noise pollution*.

nonrenewable resource (nän ri-n$\overline{oo}$′ ə bəl rē′sôrs) A resource that can't be replaced in nature. (E31) Fossil fuels such as oil and coal are *nonrenewable resources*.

nucleus (n$\overline{oo}$′klē əs) 1. The cell structure that controls all of a cell's activities. (A13) The *nucleus* was clearly visible after the cell was stained. 2. The central part of an atom, made up of protons and neutrons. (C23) The *nucleus* of a helium atom contains two protons and two neutrons.

nutrients (n$\overline{oo}$′trē ənts) Substances that are needed for an organism to live and grow. (A11) Proteins, carbohydrates, and fats are *nutrients* found in food.

octave (äk′tiv) The series of eight notes that makes up a musical scale. (F67) The music student practiced playing *octaves* on the piano.

omnivore (äm′ni vôr) A consumer that eats both plants and animals. (D16) Because they eat both meats and vegetables, many humans are *omnivores*.

opaque (ō pāk′) Not letting light through. (F46) The *opaque* curtains kept out the sunlight.

open ocean (ō′pən ō′shən) The large saltwater ecosystem containing both floating and free-swimming organisms. (D53) The *open ocean* covers much of Earth's surface.

ore (ôr) A mineral or rock that contains enough of a metal to make mining the metal profitable. (E27) Hematite is an *ore* mined for its iron content.

organ (ôr′gən) Different types of tissue working together to perform a certain function. (A12) The heart, skin, and lungs are *organs* of the human body.

organ system (ôr′gən sis′təm) Groups of organs working together. (A12) The digestive system is an *organ system* that includes the stomach, small intestine, and large intestine.

overtone (o′vər tōn) A fainter, higher tone that harmonizes with the main tone produced by a musical instrument or the human voice. (F56) The blending of *overtones* gives the flute its unique sound.

parasitism (par′ə sīt iz əm) A relationship between two organisms in which one organism lives on or in the other, feeds upon it, and usually harms it. (D19) The way in which fleas live on dogs is an example of *parasitism*.

peristalsis (per ə stal′sis) A wavelike motion that moves food through the digestive system. (A41) Swallowed food is moved through the esophagus to the stomach by means of *peristalsis*.

phonograph (fō′nə graf) A device that reproduces sounds recorded on a disk. (F88) We played old records on the *phonograph*.

photosynthesis (fōt ō sin′thə sis) The process by which producers, such as plants, make their own food by using energy from the Sun. (A19, D33) *Photosynthesis* takes place primarily in the leaves of plants.

physical change (fiz′i kəl chānj) A change in which the size, shape, or state of matter changes but no new substances are formed. (C57) Cutting an apple in half and freezing water into ice are examples of *physical change*.

physical property (fiz′i kəl präp′ər tē) A characteristic of matter that can be detected or measured with the senses. (C13) A *physical property* of a ball is its round shape.

pistil (pis′ til) The female part of a flower. (A84) Pollen grains stick to the stigma, which is at the tip of the *pistil*.

pitch (pich) The highness or lowness of a sound. (F66) A tuba produces sounds with a low *pitch*.

plane mirror (plān mir′ər) A mirror that has a flat surface. (F22) The mirror over the bathroom sink is a *plane mirror*.

planet (plan′it) A large body in space that orbits a star and does not produce light on its own. (B17) Saturn is one of nine known *planets* that revolve around the Sun.

pollen grain (pal'ən grān) A structure produced in the male part of a flower and which contains the male sex cell. (A85) The *pollen grains* of a flower must be carried from the stamen to the pistil in order for seeds to be formed.

pollination (päl ə nā'shən) The transfer of pollen grains to the pistil of a flower. (A85) Bees often help in the process of *pollination*.

population (päp yōō lā'shən) A group of the same kind of organisms that live in an area. (D8) There is a *population* of frogs in that marsh.

potential energy (pō ten'shəl en'ər jē) The energy that an object has because of its position or structure; stored energy. (C46) A coiled spring has *potential energy*.

producer (prō dōōs'ər) An organism that makes its own food through photosynthesis. (D16) Plants and algae are examples of *producers*.

protein (prō'tēn) Organic compounds that form the structure of and control the processes that take place in living things. (D39) *Proteins* provide the body with materials that help cells grow and repair themselves.

protostar (prōt'ō stär) A concentration of matter found in space that is the beginning of a star. (B64) When the temperature inside a *protostar* becomes high enough, nuclear reactions begin and the protostar turns into a star.

pulse (puls) The throbbing caused by blood rushing into the arteries when the lower chambers of the heart contract. (A57) A doctor takes a patient's *pulse* by feeling an artery in the wrist.

pupa (pyōō'pə) The stage in a life cycle between the larva and the adult. (A74) The cocoon is the *pupa* stage in the life cycle of a moth.

quarry (kwôr'ē) A mine, usually near or at Earth's surface, from which rock is removed. (E52) Granite, sandstone, limestone, slate, and marble are some rocks that come from a *quarry*.

radiation (rā dē ā'shən) The transfer of energy by waves. (C39) Energy given off by the Sun travels as *radiation* through space.

radioactive element (rā dē ō ak'tiv el'ə mənt) An element that releases energy and tiny particles from the nuclei of its atoms. (C55) Two *radioactive elements* are uranium and plutonium.

radio telescope (rā' dē ō tel'ə skōp) A gigantic antenna on Earth designed to receive radio signals from space. (B90) *Radio telescopes* are important tools for studying distant stars and galaxies.

rarefaction (rer ə fak'shən) A region in a sound wave where there are fewer particles than normal. (F55) The *rarefactions* that a vibrating violin string produces are areas of lower-than-normal air pressure.

recipient (ri sip'ē ənt) A person who receives blood in a blood transfusion. (A58) An accident victim is often the *recipient* of transfused blood.

red giant (red jī'ənt) A very large old reddish star that has greatly expanded and cooled as its fuel has begun to run out. (B65) As the Sun reaches old age, it will turn into a *red giant.*

reflecting telescope (ri flekt'iŋ tel'ə skōp) An instrument for viewing distant objects that uses a curved mirror at the back of its tube to gather light and produce an image. (B22, F39) This observatory uses a *reflecting telescope* to observe faraway galaxies.

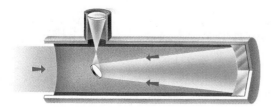

reflection (ri flek'shən) The bouncing of light from a surface. (F22) The *reflection* of sunlight off the snow made us squint.

refracting telescope (ri frakt'iŋ tel'ə skōp) An instrument for viewing distant objects that uses two lenses to gather light and produce an image. (B21, F38) The *refracting telescope* allowed a closer look at the Moon.

refraction (ri frak'shən) The bending of light as it passes from one material into another. (F24) Light traveling from air into water will undergo *refraction.*

relative age (rel'ə tiv āj) The age of an object as compared to that of other objects. (E76) The order of layers of rock shows the *relative ages* of the layers.

renewable resource (ri noo'ə bəl rē'sôrs) A resource that can be replaced in a fairly short time. (E31) Trees are considered to be *renewable resources.*

respiratory system (res'pər ə tôr ē sis'təm) The body parts that work together to take air into the body and push it back out. (A46) The lungs are the central organs in the *respiratory system.*

retina (ret''n ə) The light-sensitive area at the back of the eye on which an image is formed. (F34) The *retina* contains two kinds of cells.

revolution (rev ə loo'shən) The movement of an object around another object or point. (B13) It takes about 365 days for Earth to make one *revolution* around the Sun.

river (riv′ər) A freshwater ecosystem characterized by running water. (D50) Salmon are able to swim against the current in a *river.*

rock (räk) A solid material made of minerals that forms Earth's crust. (E40) Earth's crust is made of *rock.*

rock cycle (räk sī′kəl) The continuous series of changes that rocks undergo. (E60) In the *rock cycle,* changes are brought about by factors such as weathering, melting, cooling, or pressure.

root (r$\overline{oo}$t) The underground part of a plant that anchors the plant and absorbs water and nutrients. (A16) Carrots and turnips have one large *root.*

rotation (rō tā′shən) The spinning motion of an object on its axis. (B13) It takes about 24 hours for Earth to make one complete *rotation.*

saliva (sə lī′və) The watery liquid in the mouth that begins the chemical breakdown of food. (A38) Just the thought of food, as well as its odor and taste, will cause *saliva* to flow into the mouth.

satellite (sat′′l īt) A natural or human-built object that revolves around another object in space. (B44) The Moon is a natural *satellite* of Earth.

sediment (sed′ə mənt) Bits of weathered rocks and minerals and pieces of dead plants or animals. (E43) Over time *sediments* can form sedimentary rocks, such as sandstone and limestone.

sedimentary rock (sed ə men′tər ē räk) A type of rock that forms when sediments harden. (E43) Most *sedimentary rocks* form in layers.

semicircular canal (sem i sʉr′kyə lər kə nal′) Any of three curved tube-like structures of the inner ear that help the body to maintain balance. (F83) The *semicircular canals* respond to movements of the head.

sexual reproduction (sek′sh$\overline{oo}$ əl rē′prə duk′shən) The production of offspring that occurs when a male sex cell joins a female sex cell. (A84) The *sexual reproduction* of flowers is greatly aided by insects.

shoreline (shôr′līn) The ecosystem where land and ocean meet. (D52) Tides affect organisms that live along the *shoreline.*

simple microscope (sim′pəl mī′krə-skōp) A microscope that uses a single lens to magnify objects. (F41) A magnifying glass is a *simple microscope.*

small intestine (smôl in tes′tən) The long coiled organ where most digestion takes place. (A42) The *small intestine* is about 6 m (20 ft) long.

smelting (smelt′iŋ) The process of melting ore to remove the metal from it. (E28) Workers obtain iron by *smelting* iron ore in a blast furnace.

solar system (sō′lər sis′təm) The Sun and the planets and other objects that orbit the Sun. Also, any star and the objects that revolve around it. (B34) Our *solar system* consists of the Sun, nine known planets, and many smaller objects.

solid (säl′id) Matter that has a definite shape and a definite volume. (C21) A rock is an example of a *solid*.

solution (se lo͞o′shən) A mixture in which the different particles of matter are spread evenly. (C28) A *solution* of salt in water has some properties that are different from those of water alone.

sound (sound) A form of energy that travels through matter as waves. (F54) The *sound* made the floor vibrate.

sound synthesizer (sound sin′thə-sī zər) An electronic device that can produce a wide variety of sounds. (F69) The composer used a *sound synthesizer* to create a new musical composition.

stamen (stā′mən) The male reproductive structure of a flower. (A84) Pollen is produced in the *stamen*.

star (stär) A huge globe of hot gases that shines by its own light. (B17) Many *stars* may have systems of planets.

stem (stem) The part of a plant that supports the leaves and flowers and carries water to those parts. (A18) The trunk of a tree is a *stem*.

stomach (stum′ək) The muscular organ that stores food and helps digest it. (A41) The *stomach* squeezes and churns food into a souplike mixture called chyme.

streak (strēk) The colored powder made by rubbing a mineral against a ceramic surface. (E15) Although pyrite is yellow, it produces a black *streak*.

supernova (so͞o′pər nō və) An exploding star. (B66) When a massive red giant star uses up all its fuel, it collapses and explodes in a *supernova*.

sweat glands (swet glandz) Small coiled tubes that end at pores on the skin's surface. (A64) The *sweat glands* help to adjust the temperature of the body.

syncline (sin′klīn) A downward fold of rock layers. (E82) Forces in Earth pushing on rock formed a *syncline*.

taiga (tī′gə) A biome that contains many coniferous trees and in which rainfall is moderate. (D49) The *taiga* is south of the tundra.

terrestrial planet (tə res′trē əl plan′it) An object in space that resembles Earth in size, in density, and in its mainly rocky composition. (B44) Mars is a *terrestrial planet.*

theory (thē′ə rē) A hypothesis that is supported by a lot of evidence and is widely accepted by scientists. (S9) The big-bang *theory* offers an explanation for the origin of the universe.

timbre (tam′bər) The quality of sound that sets one voice or musical instrument apart from another. (F56) The same note played on a violin and on a trumpet differ in *timbre.*

tissue (tish′o͞o) Similar cells working together. (A12) Muscle *tissue* contains cells that contract.

trachea (trā′kē ə) The air tube that joins the throat to the lungs. (A46) Choking occurs when an object becomes stuck in the *trachea.*

translucent (trans lo͞o′sənt) Letting light through but scattering it; objects cannot be clearly seen through translucent material. (F47) The *translucent* lampshade dimmed the room.

transparent (trans per′ənt) Letting light through; objects can be clearly seen through transparent material. (F47) Window glass is usually *transparent* so that people can see through it.

tropical rain forest (träp′i kəl rān fôr′ist) A biome distinguished by lush vegetation, abundant rainfall, and plentiful sunlight. (D48) The *tropical rain forest* supports the greatest variety of life of any biome.

tropism (trō′piz əm) A growth response of a plant to conditions in the environment, such as light or water. (A24) Growing toward a light source is an example of a plant *tropism.*

trough (trôf) The low point of a wave; in a sound wave, the regions of lower air pressure. (F17, F55) A *trough* occurs between two wave crests.

tundra (tun′drə) A biome characterized by cold temperatures and low precipitation. (D49) The *tundra* blooms in summer.

universe (yo͞on′ə vʉrs) The sum of everything that exists. (B38) Our solar system is part of the *universe.*

urine (yoor′in) The yellowish liquid containing wastes and water from the filtering units of the kidneys. (A63) A doctor may test a sample of *urine* to check a patient's health.

vacuole (vak′yo͞o ōl) A cell part that stores water and nutrients. (A13) Some plant cells have large *vacuoles.*

variable (ver′ē ə bəl) The one difference in the setups of a controlled experiment; provides a comparison for testing a hypothesis. (S7) The *variable* in an experiment with plants was the amount of water given each plant.

veins (vānz) Blood vessels that carry blood from the capillaries to the heart. (A57) The walls of *veins* are thinner than those of arteries.

vertebrate (vur′tə brit) An animal with a backbone. (A76) *Vertebrates* are the large group of living things that includes mammals, fish, birds, reptiles, and amphibians.

vibration (vī brā′shən) A back-and-forth movement of matter. (F54) The *vibration* of guitar strings produces sound.

villi (vil′ī) Looplike structures in the wall of the small intestine in which nutrients are passed from the small intestine into the blood. (A43) The *villi* release mucus as well as absorb nutrients in the small intestine.

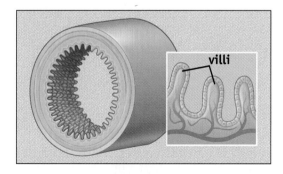

visible light (viz′ə bəl līt) A form of electromagnetic energy that can be seen. (F8) The eye responds to *visible light*.

volume (väl′yoom) 1. The amount of space an object takes up. (C10) A great *volume* of snow drifted over the road. 2. The loudness or softness of a sound. (F76) Please turn up the *volume*.

water cycle (wôt′ər sī′kəl) A continuous process in which water moves between the atmosphere and Earth's surface, including the use of water by living things. (D34) The *water cycle* is powered by energy from the Sun.

wave (wāv) A disturbance that carries energy and that travels away from its starting point. (F17) The experiment measured how quickly light *waves* travel.

wavelength (wāv′ləŋkth) The distance between one crest of a wave and the next crest. (F17, F55) Red light has a longer *wavelength* than blue light does.

weathering (weth′ər iŋ) The breaking up of rocks into sediments by such forces as wind, rain, and sunlight. (E62) Through *weathering*, igneous rock can be broken down into sediments.

wetland (wet′land) Any one of three ecosystems—marsh, swamp, or bog—where land and fresh water meet. (D51) *Wetlands* help purify water.

white dwarf (wīt dwarf) A very small dying star that gives off very little light. (B65) When the Sun's fuel runs out, it will collapse into a *white dwarf*.

INDEX

* **Activity**

CREDITS

ILLUSTRATORS
Cover: Olivia McElroy.

Think Like a Scientist: 3–4: Garry Colby. 14: Laurie Hamilton. *Border:* Olivia McElroy.

Unit A 10–11: Paul Mirocha. 13: Carlyn Iverson. 16–17: Walter Stewart. 18, 20: Steve Buchanan. 22: Carlyn Iverson. 24–25: Patrick Gnan. 28: Carlyn Iverson. 30: Richard LaRocco. 34: Leonard Morgan. 39–43, 46–50, 56–57: Richard LaRocco. 58–59: Albert Lorenz. 62–63: Richard LaRocco. 64, 66: Carlyn Iverson. 72–73: Ilene Robinette. 75: Patrick Gnan. 76: Rob Schuster. 79: Michael Maydak. 84–85: Glory Bechtold. 86–87: Catherine Deeter. 88–89: Eldon Doty. 91–92: Michael Maydak.

Unit B 9: Delores Bego. 10–11: *border* Dale Glasgow. 11: Tom Powers. 13: Jeff Hitch. 14: Michael Carroll. 15: Tony Novak. 17: Robert Schuster. 21: Lane Yerkes. 22: Fred Holz. 24–25: Jim Starr. 27: Tom Powers. 30: Dale Glasgow. 34–35: Dennis Davidson. 36: *b.m.* Dale Glasgow; *m.m.* Verlin Miller; *m.r.* Susan Melrath. 37: *t.l.* Dale Glasgow, Susan Melrath. 38–39: Michael Carroll. 42–43: Dennis Davidson. 44–49: Robert Schuster. 50: *t.r.* Dale Glasgow; *m.l.* Michael Carroll; *m.t.* Robert Schuster. 57: Tom Powers. 60–61: Lu Matthews. 64–65: Joe Spencer. 67: Tom Powers. 70: Michael Carroll. 71: Tom Powers. 72: Joe LeMonnier. 73: Tom Powers. 79: Terry Boles. 80: Stephen Wagner. 82–83: Nina Laden. 91: Andy Myer. 92: Dale Glasgow. 93: Terry Boles.

Unit C 23: Nadine Sokol. 24, 25, 29: Olivia. 31: Nadine Sokol. 40: *t.* Carolyn Bracken; *b.* Ron Fleming. 48–49: David Uhl. 50: *b.* Ka Botzis. 50–51: *t.* Sarah Jane English. 55: Eldon Doty. 56, 57: Ron Fleming. 58: *m.* Stephen Bauer; *b.* Ron Fleming, Joe Spencer. 59: *b.* Ron Fleming, Joe Spencer. 60, 61: Ron Fleming.

Unit D 8–9: Robert Hynes. 10–11: Jim Salvati. 15: Wendy Smith-Griswold. 17: Marcos Montiero. 18: Lori Anzalone. 26: David Barber. 27, 29: Andy Lendway. 32–35: Don Stewart. 36–37: Jim Starr. 39–40: Don Stewart. 41: Andy Lendway. 46–49: Rodica Prato. 50–53: Paul Mirocha. 54: Joe LeMonnier. 57: Carlos Ochagavia.

Unit E 12–16: Lingta King. 20–21: Wendy Smith-Griswold. 28: Jeanette Adams. 30–31: Bill Morse. 40: Brad Gaber. 47: Robert Pasternack. 55: Scot Ritchie. 58–59: Brad Gaber. 60: Michael Sloan. 61–63: Terry Boles. 68–69: Chuck Carter. 70: Scot Ritchie. 71: Chuck Carter. 74: Eldon Doty. 75: Carlyn Iverson. 76: *t.* Susan Melrath; *b.* Carlyn Iverson. 83: *t.* Robert Pasternack; *b.* Joe LeMonnier. 84: Verlin Miller. 85: Jim Starr. 89: Robert Pasternack. 91: Joe LeMonnier.

Unit F 8: *t.* Scot Ritchie. 8–9: *b.* Michael Carroll. 12, 13: Eldon Doty. 16: Jeanette Adams. 17, 18–19: Robert Pasternack. 18, 19: Ron Magnes. 22, 25, 26, 27: Bob Brugger. 32: J.A.K. Graphics. 33: *t., b.* Patrick Gnan, Carlyn Iverson. 34: *b.* J.A.K. Graphics, Carlyn Iverson. 35: Marie Dauenheimer. 36, 37: George Kelvin. 39: *t.* Bob Bredemeier; *b.* Eldon Doty. 43: Andy Miller. 45: Jim Fanning. 46: Len Morgan. 49: Rose Berlin. 54, 55, 57: Dale Glasgow & Assoc. 61: Terry Boles. 64–65: Tom Lochray. 66–67: *t.* Mark Bender. 66, 67: *b.* Roger Chandler. 69–70: Larry Moore. 76: *t.* Marty Bucella; *m.* Ray Vella. 76–77: *b.* Ray Vella. 83: Ellen Going Jacobs. 89, 90: Dale Gustafson. 91: Dale Glasgow & Assoc. 91–92–93: *t.* Dale Glasgow & Assoc. 92: *m.* Tim Blough. 95: Patrick Gnan.

Math and Science Toolbox: *Logos:* Nancy Tobin. 14–15: Andrew Shiff. *Borders:* Olivia McElroy.

Glossary 19: Ellen Going Jacobs. 20: Robert Margulies. 21: Fran Milner. 23: Tom Powers. 26: Carlyn Iverson. 28: Richard Larocca. 29, 31: Robert Pasternack. 33: Gary Torrisi. 37: Robert Margulies.

PHOTOGRAPHS
All photographs by Houghton Mifflin Co. (HMCo.) unless otherwise noted.

Front Cover: *t.* Superstock; *m.l.* G.K. & Vikki Hart/The Image Bank; *m.r.* Runk/Schoenberger/Grant Heilman Photography, Inc.; *b.l.* NASA/Media Services; *b.r.* Superstock.

Think Like a Scientist: 2: *b.* Chip Porter/Tony Stone Images. 3: *t.* Paul Seheult, Eye Ubiquitous/Corbis. 10: *b. bkgd.* PhotoDisc, Inc.

Table of Contents vii: *l.* Anglo-Australian Observatory; *m.l.* © Royal Observatory, Edinburgh/AATB/Science Photo Library/Photo Researchers, Inc.; *m.r.* © Royal Observatory, Edinburgh/AATB/Science Photo Library/Photo Researchers, Inc.; *r.* MGA/Photri, Inc. x: *t.* J.C. Carton/Bruce Coleman Incorporated; *m.* J.C. Carton/Bruce Coleman Incorporated; *b.* Michael Fogden/Bruce Coleman Incorporated. xi: DN Metalsmith. xii: *inset* E.R. Degginger/Color-Pic, Inc.; *bkgd.* E.R. Degginger/Color-Pic, Inc.; *b.* E.R. Degginger/Color-Pic, Inc.; *r.* Doug Sokell/Tom Stack & Associates. xiv: © Cecil Fox/Science Photo Library/Photo Researchers, Inc.

Unit A 1: Prof. P. Motta/Dept. of Anatomy/University "La Sapienza", Rome/Science Photo Library/Custom Medical Stock Photo, Inc. 2–3: Prof. P. Motta/Dept. of Anatomy/University "La Sapienza", Rome/Science Photo Library/Custom Medical Stock Photo, Inc. 4–5: *bkgd* Ron Garrison/The Zoological Society of San Diego; *inset* Ken Kelley for HMCo. 7: *t.m.* Clive Druett; Papilio/Corbis Corporation; *b.m.* Kim Sayer/Corbis Corporation; *b.r.* Mitchell Gerber/Corbis Corporation; *b.l.* E.R. Degginger/Color-Pic, Inc. 9: Ken Karp for HMCo. 10: *l.* E.R. Degginger/Color-Pic, Inc.; *inset* Don & Pat Valenti/DRK Photo. 12: *t.* © P. Dayanandan/Photo

Krasemann/DRK Photo. 56: *t.l.* J.C. Carton/Bruce Coleman Incorporated; *t.r.* J.C. Carton/Bruce Coleman Incorporated; *m.l.* Michael Fogden/Animals Animals/Earth Scenes; *m.r.* Thomas R. Fletcher/Stock Boston; *b.* Michael Fogden/Bruce Coleman Incorporated. 58: *t.* Michael Fogden/DRK Photo; *b.* Greg Vaughn/Tom Stack & Associates. 59: Mark Carwardine/Still Pictures/Peter Arnold, Inc. 60: *l.* BIOS/Peter Arnold, Inc.; *r.* David Dennis/Tom Stack & Associates. 61: *t.* B. Herrod OSF/Animals Animals/Earth Scenes; *m.l.* Stephen J. Krasemann/Peter Arnold, Inc.; *m.r.* Norbert Wu/Peter Arnold, Inc.; *b.* R. Andrew Odum/Peter Arnold, Inc.

Unit E 1: Joseph Sohm/ChromoSohm Inc./Corbis Corporation. 2–3: Joseph Sohm/ChromoSohm Inc./Corbis Corporation. 4: DN Metalsmith. 4–5: *bkgd.* JLM Visuals; *inset* DN Metalsmith. 5: DN Metalsmith. 6–7: Grant Huntington for HMCo. 8: Grant Huntington for HMCo. 8–9: Grant Huntington for HMCo. 9: *t.* Grant Huntington for HMCo.; *b.* Grant Huntington for HMCo. 10: Grant Huntington for HMCo. 12: *m.l.* Joy Spurr/Bruce Coleman Incorporated; *m.r.* E.R. Degginger/Color-Pic, Inc. 13: *l.* E.R. Degginger/Bruce Coleman Incorporated; *r.* Runk/Schoenberger/Grant Heilman Photography, Inc. 15: *t.* Grant Huntington for HMCo.; *b.l.* Runk/Schoenberger/Grant Heilman Photography, Inc.; *m.b.* E.R. Degginger/Color-Pic, Inc.; *b.r.* Breck P. Kent Photography. 16: *t.* Runk/Schoenberger/Grant Heilman Photography, Inc.; *b.* E.R. Degginger/Color-Pic, Inc. 17: *b.l.* Grant Huntington for HMCo.; *m.b.* Grant Huntington for HMCo.; *b.r.* Grant Huntington for HMCo. 18: *l.* Grant Huntington for HMCo.; *m.* Grant Huntington for HMCo.; *r.* Grant Huntington for HMCo. 21: *l.* Breck P. Kent Photography; *m.* © Bill Bachman/Photo Researchers, Inc.; *r.* © Phillip Hayson/Photo Researchers, Inc. 23: Grant Huntington for HMCo. 24: *l.* Runk/Schoenberger/Grant Heilman Photography, Inc.; *m.l.* I.S. Stepanowicz/Bruce Coleman Incorporated; *m.r.* Doug Sokell/Visuals Unlimited; *r.* © Roberto De Gugliemo/Science Photo Library/Photo Researchers, Inc. 25: *t.l.* E.R. Degginger/Color-Pic, Inc.; *t.r.* Chuck O'Rear/Corbis; *b.* Runk/Schoenberger/Grant Heilman Photography, Inc. 26: *t.m.* Phil Degginger/Color-Pic, Inc.; *t.r.* © 2000 Chuck O'Rear/Woodfin Camp & Associates. 27: *l.* © Gerard Vandystadt/Photo Researchers, Inc.; *m.* © Christian Grzimek/Photo Researchers, Inc.; *r.* © 2000 George Hall/Woodfin Camp & Associates. 29: *t.* © David Guyon/Science Photo Library/Photo Researchers, Inc.; *m.* Chuck O'Rear/Corbis; *b.* © James Holmes/Photo Researchers, Inc. 31: Bruce Forster/Tony Stone Images. 32: Myrleen Ferguson Cate/PhotoEdit. 33: Barry L. Runk/Grant Heilman Photography, Inc. 34–35: *bkgd.* © Chromosohm/Joe Sohm/Photo Researchers, Inc. 36–37: Grant Huntington for HMCo. 37: Grant Huntington for HMCo. 41: *t.* Phil Degginger/Color-Pic, Inc. 42: *l.* E.R. Degginger/Color-Pic, Inc.; *m.* Doug Sokell/Tom Stack & Associates; *r.* E.R. Degginger/Color-Pic, Inc.; *inset* E.R. Degginger/Color-Pic, Inc. 43: *l.* E.R. Degginger/Color-Pic, Inc.; *r.* E.R. Degginger/Color-Pic, Inc. 44: *t.* E.R. Degginger/Color-Pic, Inc.; *t. inset* E.R. Degginger/Color-Pic, Inc.; *b.l.* E.R. Degginger/Color-Pic, Inc.; *b. inset* E.R. Degginger/Color-Pic, Inc.; *b.r.* Richard Hutchings for HMCo. 46: *t.l.* Tom & Susan Bean, Inc.; *m.t.* © 2000 Gary Braasch/Woodfin Camp & Associates; *m.b.* Doug Sokell/Tom Stack & Associates; *b.* Stephen Trimble Photography. 46–47: E.R. Degginger/Color-Pic, Inc. 48: *l.* E.R. Degginger/Color-Pic, Inc.; *m.* E.R. Degginger/Color-Pic, Inc.; *r.* Breck P. Kent Photography. 49: *inset* Breck P. Kent Photography; *l.* Breck P. Kent Photography; *r.* E.R. Degginger/Color-Pic, Inc. 52: *l.* © Guy Gilette/Photo Researchers, Inc.; *m.* E.R. Degginger/Color-Pic, Inc.; *r.* E.R. Degginger/Color-Pic, Inc. 52–53: Steven Frame/Stock Boston. 54: Reagan Bradshaw/The Image Bank. 55: *t.* Brick Institute of America; *m.* Brick Institute of America; *b.* Brick Institute of America. 56: Grant Huntington for HMCo. 57: Grant Huntington for HMCo. 58: *l.* Breck P. Kent Photography; *r.* Breck P. Kent Photography. 59: *l.* Breck P. Kent Photography; *r.* Breck P. Kent Photography. 62: James Watt/Animals Animals/Earth Scenes. 64: Courtesy, Rufus Catchings. 64–65: *bkgd.* Robert Frerck/Tony Stone Images; *b.* Angie Williams/U.S. Geological Survey. 72: Grant Huntington for HMCo. 73: Grant Huntington for HMCo. 74: *l.* The Granger Collection, New York; *r.* The Natural History Museum, London. 76: Breck P. Kent Photography. 77: Tom Bean/The Stock Market. 78: Grant Huntington for HMCo. 78–79: Grant Huntington for HMCo. 80: *l.* Grant Huntington for HMCo.; *r.* Grant Huntington for HMCo. 81: © Bill Bachman/Photo Researchers, Inc. 82: Grant Huntington for HMCo. 83: Michael P. Gadomski/Bruce Coleman Incorporated. 85: *t.* Lee Foster/Bruce Coleman Incorporated; *b.* Jewel Cave National Monument/US Department of the Interior, National Park Service. 86: Grant Huntington for HMCo. 87: Grant Huntington for HMCo. 88: Trevor Wood/The Image Bank. 89: Tom & Susan Bean, Inc. 90: Myrleen Ferguson Cate/PhotoEdit. 91: Paul X. Scott/Sygma Photo News. 92: Alan Pitcairn/Grant Heilman Photography, Inc.

Unit F 1: © Tom Myers/Photo Researchers, Inc. 2–3: © Tom Myers/Photo Researchers, Inc. 4: Courtesy, Richard Green/Wildfire, Inc. 4–5: *bkgd.* Dan McCoy/Rainbow; *inset* Ian Howarth. 5: Ian Howarth. 9: *l.* Paul Silverman/Fundamental Photographs; *r.* Richard Megna/Fundamental Photographs. 10: *t.* Bob Krist/Tony Stone Images. 11: *l.* Richard Megna/Fundamental Photographs; *m.* Robert Campbell; *r.* J. Pickerell/The Image Works Incorporated. 13: *t.* Stock Montage, Inc.; *b.* Culver Pictures, Inc. 16: Ebet Roberts. 17: James H. Karales/Peter Arnold, Inc. 22: *r.* Richard Hutchings. 23: *l.* Alan Oddie/PhotoEdit; *r.* David Phillips for HMCo. 24: H.R. Bramaz/Peter Arnold, Inc. 26: John M. Dunay/Fundamental Photographs. 34: *l.* Richard Megna/Fundamental Photographs; *r.* Richard Megna/Fundamental Photographs. 38: *l.* Art Resource, NY; *r.* © Dr. Jeremy Burgess/Science Photo Library/Photo Researchers, Inc. 39: *l.* Corbis Corporation; *r.* Corbis Corporation. 40: *l.* FPG International; *r.* William E. Sauro/NYT Pictures. 41: *l.* Image Select; *r.* Image Select. 42: *t.l.* © Dr. Jeremy Burgess/Science Photo Library/Photo Researchers, Inc.; *t.r.* © Cecil Fox/Science Photo Library/Photo Researchers, Inc. 43: CNRI/Science Photo Library/Custom Medical Stock Photo, Inc.; *r.* Stanley Flegler/Visuals Unlimited. 48: *t.* Diane Schiumo/Fundamental Photographs; *b.* Comstock. 50–51: *bkgd.* Paul Warchol/Sonic Architecture, Bill & Mary Buchen; *inset* Paul Warchol/Sonic Architecture, Bill & Mary Buchen. 55: *l.* Comstock; *r.* James Darell/Tony Stone Images. 57: *l.* Comstock; *r.* Comstock. 60: Stephen Green/Focus On Sports. 64: *r.* S.R.H. Spicer/The Shrine to Music Museum University of South Dakota. 65: *b.l.* S.R.H. Spicer/The Shrine to Music Museum University of South Dakota; *b.r.* S.R.H. Spicer/The Shrine to Music Museum University of South Dakota. 66: *l.* Grant Huntington for HMCo.; *r.* Richard Hutchings. 70: Spencer Grant/Stock Boston. 72: Philips Hearing Instruments. 72–73: *bkgd.* F. Scott Schafer, Photographer; *inset* Philips Hearing Instruments. 78: *t.* Ebet Roberts. 79: *l.* Jeffrey Aaronson/Network Aspen; *r.* Mary Kate Denny/PhotoEdit. 84: Corbis Corporation. 85: *r.* Visuals Unlimited. 88: *t.* Corbis Corporation; *b.* Brown Brothers. 91: Phil Jason/Tony Stone Images.

Science and Math Toolbox 2: *r.* Grant Huntington for HMCo

Glossary 24: S. Nielsen/Imagery. 27: Doug Sokell/Tom Stack & Associates. 30: MGA/Photri, Inc. 32: © Guy Gilette/Photo Researchers, Inc. 34: E.R. Degginger/Color-Pic, Inc. 35: *b.* © James Holmes/Photo Researchers, Inc. 36: USGS, Flagstaff, Arizona/Corbis Corporation.